10-13(4)
4-17(8)

DEC 17 2012

LOUISE: AMENDED

to my family

Published by Black Balloon Publishing
www.blackballoonpublishing.com

ISBN-13: 978-1-936787-01-2

Black Balloon Publishing titles are distributed to the trade by
Consortium Book Sales and Distribution
Phone: 800-283-3572 / SAN 631-760X

Library of Congress Control Number: 2011938591

Printed in the United States of America

9 8 7 6 5 4 3 2 1

FIRST EDITION

LOUISE: **AMENDED**

A MEMOIR

LOUISE KRUG

BLACK BALLOON PUBLISHING ⦿ BROOKLYN

CONTENTS

PART ONE:

THE INCIDENT

CHAPTER ONE

Two weeks before it happened, my boyfriend Claude hooked me up with the West Coast editor of *Us magazine*. The editor said she might have some work for me. Britney Spears and her husband Kevin Federline were rumored to be on their way to Santa Barbara. Could I meet a reporter from the magazine, Evan, at the Four Seasons resort in one hour?

I wore a red dress. I'd coated my long, blond hair with a silicone sheen, and worn the heels everyone was wearing that year: pointy, naked on the sides, ankle straps. Evan said Wow when I walked up to him in the lobby. He gave me my mission as we sat at the hotel bar: Follow Britney around for two days, gather any information I could, and don't get caught. I would be paid $300 a day, $500 a day on weekends, to answer a list of questions. Was she pregnant? Did she smoke? What did she eat? Any cellulite? etc. Evan had been covering Britney for years and couldn't get too close without being recognized. I was a pretty girl with an unknown face—not unusual for the Four Seasons resort in Santa Barbara. I would not stand out.

Evan and I stood on the lawn beneath the lit window of her suite. We could see the blue light from a TV.

"They're probably fucking. See you tomorrow," he said.

Early the next morning I was back at the hotel with everything Evan had told me to bring: a few changes of clothes to minimize recognition; sunglasses and a bikini; a notepad and pen. I was more nervous than I'd ever been. I coached myself during the drive there. I wanted to hear it said out loud, that this was really happening. That I had gotten this chance.

I was twenty-two. I'd just moved to Santa Barbara from Kansas. This opportunity was as big as I'd known how to dream at the time.

I went to the salon where Britney had received a pedicure the afternoon before. I got one too, and pretended to be a starstruck fan. I pumped the manicurist for insights. Instead I got talked into an expensive eyebrow wax.

I overheard someone say that Britney was at a nearby wig shop, so I ran there, slowed down at the door, and walked casually inside. She was trying a few on: a red bob with bangs; a black Elvira wig that went halfway down her back. Later I found myself sneaking into the resort pool and stretching out on a towel several cabanas away. She was tanning and, I noted, fanning herself with a little red Kabbalah book. My triumph was to be seated one table over at lunch. I watched her eat a salad with ranch dressing, smoke many cigarettes, and drink six lemonades. I watched a waiter ask her to please put a shirt over her bikini top. I watched her talk on the phone and belch loudly. Evan ran back and forth across the street on the sidewalk giving me a thumb's up.

I had Claude meet me at the Four Seasons restaurant for a $200 dinner we couldn't afford, hoping Britney would show up. She didn't. The next morning I sat on a bench and watched the bellboys load up her white Lexus, telling myself to ask a question, any question, to run up and tug on her ponytail to see if it came off. I couldn't speak or move.

That afternoon I typed up all of my notes and emailed them to the magazine editor. I never got paid but my name is there, in the February 7, 2005 edition of *Us magazine*, tiny, practically invisible, at the end.

If I believed in God, I might say that what happened next saved me from a trivial life of empty goals and frivolous dreams. But I don't believe in God, so there goes that.

CHAPTER TWO

A nurse calls my name from the waiting list. My right leg is completely numb. Claude has to help me out of my chair. I shakily tell her my symptoms, even though she can plainly see what is wrong:

1) Leg drags behind me
2) Hand cannot lift a cup to my lips
3) Eyes won't look at the same thing at the same time

While recounting these problems I begin to cry and cannot stop, even after she cradles me for a second, after she lifts me onto a bed to wait for the doctor. This isn't supposed to be happening, I think. I've only been in California for two months. Right now I'm supposed to be at my first day of work, as a reporter for a local paper, my first job out of college. For the interview I'd bought a form-fitting striped pantsuit and crocodile stilettos. On the way to the interview I'd stopped for a latte and a business magazine and felt smart and adult. My answers had come out of my mouth like someone had pressed a button. The editor had sports analogies for me. He wanted a reporter who would hit home runs and catch fly balls with the sun shining in their eyes. I said I could. I'd spent a hundred dollars on makeup and learned how to apply it on a department store stool and it had obviously been worth it.

Obviously.

The doctor starts giving me reflex tests, tapping my knees with a little hammer. I can see that my right side is not reacting as it should. He tells the nurse to order an MRI. I tell myself I will soon be out of this emergency room and on my way to work. After all, it is a sunny Monday in California. Nothing bad can happen here, the weather is too good, the people, too rich.

CHAPTER THREE

The night before it happens they are at a movie premiere. Claude is a reporter for a local paper and has been assigned to cover the Santa Barbara Film Festival. Louise has a reporting job as well—she will cover gardens, weddings, and pets for another publication—but her job doesn't start until the next day.

The theater is outdoors with roaming spotlights and palm trees. Louise is tall with long, blond hair and big eyes. Claude wears gel in his hair and leaves his shirt mostly unbuttoned. People look at them. They like to be photographed together. Their refrigerator is covered with pictures that fall down every time someone walks by.

The movie ends and as they walk up the aisle, Louise falls on a woman behind her. Claude helps Louise out of the way so the annoyed woman can get by. Louise takes off a spiky shoe and stares at her toes. She has bought a new outfit for the occasion, tight black pants and a sleeveless, lacy top.

"I can't feel anything," she says.

On the way to the parking garage Louise drags her right foot as if a child were hanging on her leg. People stare. Claude thinks it is a bit much.

They agree that she must have sat the wrong way during the movie. Claude needs to write his review of the premiere and file before dawn. They drive back to their apartment, eat a frozen pizza, and try not to think too much.

In the morning Louise is too dizzy to stand. The noise of the shower is so loud against the plastic curtain she cannot go inside. She hangs on the towel rack, and Claude tries to hold her up so the rod doesn't snap. On the way to the emergency room Louise is crying that the sound of horns and tires against pavement is killing her, but the windows are already rolled up. He pulls her against his chest, and covers her ear with one hand as he drives.

•

Claude is anxious. He is anxious about Louise and anxious about work. He writes for the Montecito paper, covering neighborhood-watch programs, charity functions, and clubhouse rules. His boss, who used to be in the pornography business, is his best friend's father. He trusts Claude to tell him which letters to the editor are worthy of a response. Most concern the lack of good security guards in the village. Montecito is a tiny village near Santa Barbara where only the very rich can afford to live. It is on the coast with gated mansions and golf carts. The inventor of Beanie Babies lives there, as do Oprah and Michael Douglas. Couples sit in restaurant gardens with their big dogs and drink tequila served on beds of ice. Personal chefs and nutritionists keep their insides clean. The women wear gold, ropy jewelry with giant stones that absorb the sun. The paper is free, available in metal containers around the town, by the bakery or gelato shop.

They have been sitting in the ER for hours with no word. Louise keeps telling him to go. His boss is waiting. It is a good job, she says.

•

My uncle Charlie is here. He lives close by, and the rest of my family is a plane ride away. The nurses had said the MRI results would take hours, so I told Claude he could go to work, that I'd feel more carefree without him here.

I didn't think he'd believe me.

My uncle is wearing a dove-colored suit. His smooth blue

tie is cool to the touch. He covers his nose at the smell of the hospital, at the odor coming from the other side of the curtain where someone is screaming. "Let's get out of here," he says, looking around for an exit.

We are called into the doctor's office. The doctor turns off the lights and shows us the MRI results on a lit screen. He points to a marble-sized white spot at the base of my brain, near the neck. The white spot is blood, he says.

This is sounding familiar. When I was nine a blood vessel burst in the pons region of my brain stem, but there had been few side effects, and the blood had reabsorbed after a couple of months. The doctor says it has happened again, and this time it is more severe. The blood is putting pressure on the pons, which controls functions like breathing and swallowing. The reason I have not died is that the cavernous angioma has only bled a little bit. Not enough to stop my functions totally. Everything may reabsorb again, he says. Who knows, I could wake up tomorrow and feel all better. He refers me to a team of doctors in a Los Angeles hospital, which is more equipped to deal with this kind of thing. For now, he says, I should just go home. He gives me some pain-killers from his pocket.

Uncle Charlie and I go to the hospital cafeteria before we leave. We make fun of the doctor. We eat sticky carrot salad and turkey on whole wheat. My uncle calls my father, and I call my mother, who says she will board the first plane. I tell her not to worry, but she says she is my mother, of course she is coming. My uncle drives me home in his elegant car and I feel calm. From the pills, mostly.

•

Claude is stuck in late-morning traffic on the highway. He watches the ocean and thinks about how much he likes Louise, and how much he hopes that whatever's wrong with her isn't serious, because he has never helped anyone through anything, not really. Most people haven't, he guesses. He wonders if he will know what to do when the time comes, and if it will be enough.

•

The next day everything is worse. I try to get ready for work in a white skirt and a silky top that glows like lava, but the numbness has spread to my right hand and I can't button anything. I go back to bed and lie down. Claude is still sleeping. I cannot miss another day of work. I cannot spend another day at the ER when I'm supposed to be outside on the sand with a tape recorder, covering Japanese teenagers out surfing for the first time. Or in the farmers' market, trailing Spaniards and Germans, asking them what they think of American hot dogs. Delicious, yes? We are all Californian now!

An ambulance takes me to Los Angeles.

•

This has been manageable until the ambulance. It was manageable yesterday with my uncle in the cafeteria, and at home, with Claude. But now a man puts a tube in my nose and tells me to breathe in. Now I know it is serious. Now I know something very wrong is going on.

I don't want to tell the nurses in LA about the double vision because this makes my case sound much worse than I want it to be. I pretend my left eye has not turned inward. I pretend the right side of my body does not feel full of sand. I pretend this is not me, that this is happening to someone else, and it almost works. When a nurse inserts a needle into my right arm I almost don't feel it.

The doctor sweeps into the room. He says the cavernous angioma must be cut out of my brain immediately. The operation, called a craniotomy, is very dangerous, but the lesion cannot be shrunk by radiation, or the pons will suffer. It cannot be cut out by a gamma knife, because the slightest error could kill me. And it cannot be left alone because chances are it will bleed again—no one knows how much or when. Another bleed could be fatal. Surgery is the only option. The neurosurgeon will be back in town in two days. I must wait, here, in the hospital.

I become hysterical. The nurse injects me with a tranquilizer that makes me claw at my skin, and I try to leave the room, dragging all of my tubes along. Nurses hold me down.

My mother arrives and gets into bed with me, smelling like plane. She is small and fits well. Her name is Janet and she lives in Kansas. She wears practical clothes, leather sandals with socks, jeans, and T-shirts. She is the publisher of the town newspaper and is the boss of some people. When I was growing up, she was one of the best players on our town's tennis team. She has a boyfriend. She leaves the hot, dim room to find a wet washcloth for my face.

By the time Claude arrives it has been dark for a long time. It is an hour and a half from Montecito to Los Angeles. He apologizes. The newspaper, he explains. The traffic. He's so sorry.

•

For two days my mother and I watch the mounted hospital TV. Finally, the neurosurgeon we've been waiting for returns from a conference in Sweden. He says he cannot perform the craniotomy, at least not right away. He wants to consult some other specialists. Mom and I think he's stalling, covering his ass, afraid of lawsuits. I am told to wait for a phone call. It will take about a week.

Claude picks us up outside the hospital and waits with the engine running. I am in a wheelchair. Claude has brought sunglasses because the bright sunlight hurts my eyes and face. The engine sounds like a drill inside my skull so my mother puts soundproof headphones over my ears. I do not know if my mother and Claude talk or not. They have only met a few times. I don't know much of anything right now, only that we are driving out of Los Angeles and along the coast back to our apartment in Santa Barbara, and that every minute it is getting worse.

CHAPTER FOUR

I was on the student newspaper at the University of Kansas before any of this happened. I liked journalism, though I was bad at it. Careless. As a reporter, I wrote stories on athletes volunteering at soup kitchens and fashion trends like the Brazilian bikini wax and low-rise jeans. I quoted my roommates instead of talking to strangers like I was supposed to. I rarely took the extra step to look up a word in a dictionary or check a calendar. I was used to getting by on my looks. I was used to not having to care too much.

The paper came out at midnight, and every morning the journalism professor who oversaw the operation would pin a copy on a bulletin board in the newsroom. He would have marked every mistake with a red pen; the really bad ones in green. Ones that meant *libel!* were underlined in black. Sometimes "good" was written by someone's byline. I loved that moment, when we crowded around the bulletin board to see what kind of job we had done. I liked getting chips at the vending machine and sharing cigarettes with everyone out back by the dumpster, laughing about something, usually something someone had done while drunk.

I went to lots of staff parties, and there was lots of drinking, and lots of regrettable sex. We did what people do when they work together day after day, barely out of their teenage years—stupid things. I stole another girl's boyfriend at least once, and wore a fringed leather jacket everywhere. We made up group dances at bars after late-night copy-editing shifts. After concerts I'd crowd in tiny backstage rooms with shaggy band members, and as we all smoked pot, I'd scribble quotes on gum wrappers from my purse. I threw lots of parties, themed, usually. Expected ones, like disco and white trash. The best was prom, where everyone wore their old dress or tux. Mine was light blue stiff taffeta with a full bubble skirt. I was the kind of girl other girls only pretended to like.

I grew up in the Midwest, restless, thinking I was meant for something different. Something better. We all did.

CHAPTER FIVE

C laude knows Louise from the student paper. They work together in a small stone building in the center of campus. After flirting with him for months, Louise finally invites him over for dinner. She's sexy and bronze from a spring break trip to Jamaica, where she says she broke up with her boyfriend, an older guy named Davy, who has a band and no job. Claude likes Louise, but does not want to send a message that he will be an easy, obedient boyfriend like all the others. Louise knows guys love her, he can tell from watching her sail around the newsroom, looking back to see which guys she imagines are watching her hips. He's heard things about her, that she dumps guys after two months and drinks whiskey out of a red plastic cup, and that all the professors in the journalism school think she's a slacker who comes to class hung over with a giant bottle of water and writes "filler" stories with pretty art that land on the front page. Claude saw Louise with her last boyfriend, once, in the grocery store—she'd been talking on the phone while he trailed behind her, not objecting when she tossed a bunch of dried fruit and gluten-free cookies into the cart.

"Maybe I'll come," Claude tells Louise. "Won't know for sure until the last minute."

Louise shares a soggy bungalow with two friends, and when Claude walks in, half an hour late, it smells like incense and floor cleaner and her roommates are not there. Louise is making sushi, and the rolls are big and lumpy. Claude paces the kitchen, talking on his cell phone, and Louise continues to assemble the meal alone, slicing and arranging, probably waiting for him to help her or tell her how pretty she looks. She's evidently used to guys who walk right up and cup her small face in their hands. Claude tries not to watch her. He tells himself, Don't touch.

During dinner she banters, scooting her chair so close, letting him look right down her white V-neck T-shirt to the little yellow bow on her bra, that he gives in and kisses her.

Claude doesn't call the next day. Or the next. After he graduates he's moving to California and will meet tons of girls, models, probably. Because of his mother, Claude speaks French, which has helped him always have a girlfriend. In Santa Barbara he has a job waiting for him, writing for a local paper, and will soon be really doing something, not sitting around in this wheat-filled state with these farm kids.

•

All semester, Louise has been watching Claude. He tells funny stories that the staff pass all around the newsroom. "Did you hear Claude's latest?" they ask, referring mostly to his ex-girlfriends, who are all beautiful, but troubled—one had shown up at his apartment in the middle of the night, crying and supposedly holding a pink teddy bear. The collars of Claude's shirts are always popped up, his sleeves rolled, hands gesturing while he talks. He's not the type to sulk in the kitchen at parties, hiding behind his hair while he nurses a bottle of Pabst the way Davy would. Davy's neediness embarrassed Louise. Claude she'll have to work for.

•

Claude runs into Louise at a party and finds himself leaving with her. Soon they are together for whole weekends, in her bedroom, watching TV and leafing through magazines. He loves spending time with Louise, how she looks at him, how quick she is to laugh, but he can't stand her friends, how they order blue drinks at clubs and dance crudely, spilling on themselves, and is glad when he graduates. He likes the longing that distance creates. He likes sharing dreams via email, seeing their plans typed up on a computer screen. They joke about their future apartment, one with a shiny chrome kitchen and floor-to-ceiling windows where they will stir-fry things in woks and drink sparkling wine. At night the hills of Santa Barbara will glitter with lights from outdoor living rooms and yards called "grounds." They will do yoga on a sunny balcony with cacti in pots, and drink water with fresh-squeezed lime. Louise will walk down the clean, white sidewalks with arms full of shopping bags.

Louise arrives on New Year's Eve, 2005, and for one month their lives are not so far from this. They drink Mexican beer and wear bathing suits indoors. They do drugs and wander through organic markets, spotting celebrities. They wear aviator sunglasses and fearlessly turn their faces toward the sky. Their apartment complex is called Summerville.

This would be their life now. That is what they believed.

CHAPTER SIX

When Janet's daughter was in the fourth grade, she collapsed at a Civil War site in Alabama. They were coming back from a family vacation in the Gulf Shores, famous for the squeaky sand. They had stayed in a high-rise condominium and swum in salty water for a week, and were now crowded in the station wagon again, pushing up north to their home in Michigan. This was before the divorce. Janet and Warner both wore gold rings and took turns driving. The children—Louise, Tom, and the baby, Michael— were sunburnt, and sipping apple juice from small tin cans. Warner had wanted to take a break and see a battlefield, so they had stopped at sunset. The air outside was so hot it made them pink, their stomachs and scalps stung with sweat. Then, right there in the graveyard, nine-year-old Louise fell and balled up on the scratchy yellow grass. She said she saw double and had a headache so bad she couldn't move. For a second, Janet thought Louise was psychic, feeling the pains of those killed beneath her. Then she saw that Louise's left eye had turned toward her nose. She couldn't walk straight; Warner had to guide her to the car. Janet followed, carrying the baby and holding Tom's sticky hand. He was five, silent and staring. Janet could do nothing.

At first the doctors had thought Louise had a brain tumor. Then they said no: It was a clot of blood pressing down on her brain stem, a genetic irregularity. Their prescription: complete bed rest to allow the blood to reabsorb into her brain. She had to miss the last three months of fourth grade, but her symptoms all went away. Her eye rolled back to the center and locked there. In gymnastics, she could walk across a balance beam. The blood was gone. She was allowed to go to summer camp with her friends, but the doctors had said she should abstain from "contact sports" just to be safe. She ran track. Not much was mentioned about it in the family again, except every so often, someone would say how strange it all had been.

CHAPTER SEVEN

A fter four days in the critical care unit in LA, I'm back in Santa Barbara. Back in our apartment. I have to wear an eye patch. Claude calls me Captain Hook. I call him a jerk. He says he's just trying to make things around here a little more lighthearted. My mother buys patches in pink, blue, and beige, but I never wear them. I wonder where she got these, in the costume aisle at some specialty drugstore?

The eye patch helps me not see double. Without the eye patch, I cannot tell which of the two doorknobs is real. I hold a glass under the faucet, but it will not fill up. It's like being very drunk, or like a baby, trying to walk.

CHAPTER EIGHT

J anet knows she has done something wrong. She should have worried about Louise more. She didn't call Louise for a week after she moved to California—she had wanted Louise to feel like a grown-up. Maybe she fed Louise bad foods when she was a baby?

Claude is thinking that this has happened because he has bad luck. He is always wrecking cars and losing things. He got picked on in grade school, and is short. He has a string of ex-girlfriends who hate him.

•

Janet leaves the apartment to buy a vacuum cleaner. The carpet has a lot of sand in it from the beach. The building is on a steep dirt hill overlooking four lanes of speeding cars, and then there is the water and sand. The apartment is designed like a motel, with the bedroom window looking directly onto a walkway and the parking lot. In place of a curtain, Claude and Louise have pinned a large piece of tie-dyed fabric over the bedroom window. More privacy is needed.

Janet gets off the freeway at Wagon Wheel Circle. She goes fast, around and around the wagon wheel, until she sees her exit. In the vacuum aisle of the superstore she talks to herself, observing the qualities of one device over another, and buys the best vacuum. What else would her daughter like? She picks up a little picture frame, a cinnamon candle.

For dinner, Janet steams three artichokes and beats butter, eggs, and hot pepper sauce in a bowl. She warms the mixture over the tiny electric stove. Artichokes and hollandaise sauce has been Louise's favorite meal since she was small. In Kansas, Janet is so busy that she mainly eats cereal and bananas, cold cuts and cheese, shrimp with cocktail sauce. But that is OK. This is the food she likes.

Janet and Claude get Louise out of bed. The sedatives have made her spacey and somber. Janet and Claude work together quietly, pushing and pulling Louise gently. They act as a team. Janet thinks Claude is holding up well. He goes to the grocery store and picks up around the apartment. He wants to help Louise take a bath before they eat. She hasn't been washed since the movie premiere—four days ago.

They slide her off of the bed and her pants bunch, exposing her underwear. "Don't look!" she says, and Janet almost laughs. The sheets are expensive looking, with large, purple flowers, a gift from Claude's French mom. The mattress is just a few weeks old, one of Louise and Claude's joint purchases. Now Louise clings to it. She doesn't want to go anywhere, she says. Janet and Claude soothe her with promises of warm water and bubbles. Janet feels like she is assisting her grandmother at the nursing home, Louise is that lost, that scared.

Janet waits on the balcony, watching the water and the cars. She wonders what Claude thinks of her beautiful baby now—helpless, naked, wall-eyed—

•

Claude tries to shave Louise's legs but gives up after a few strokes. She keeps squirming, it is too dangerous. Although lighter in pounds, she is dead weight, he thinks. She is scaring him as she sits in the water with her deep slouch. He is embarrassed to see that her stomach has rolls. She has never smelled like this before, like an animal. She says she wants him to wash her face, but cries when the cleanser hits. She covers her face. Her hair looks like a wig, stiff and rough. Claude spots moles on her body that he has never known about. He gently pushes her head back to get it wet. She resists. She keeps repeating for him to hurry, hurry. Her teeth chatter. Claude can find nowhere to put her but on the toilet seat. He wraps her hair in a towel and guides her into clean underwear, sweatpants, and his college T-shirt.

At the dinner table, Claude and Janet dip artichoke leaves into yellow sauce and scrape them with their teeth. Louise eats slowly, moving the leaves to her mouth with her one good hand, not talking, concentrating. They eat on a card table Claude and Louise had bought in a box set from a furniture warehouse. The chairs are small and splintery. Claude remembers their first night in this apartment just over one month ago, when Louise arrived. They'd slept on the floor in sleeping bags, all of their boxes still packed around them, a young couple just starting out.

After they put Louise to bed, Claude wants to read his current events magazine on the living room couch, but Janet is brushing her teeth in the kitchen sink and wearing her nightgown. Claude takes his magazine out to his car. He calls his sister.

"Why don't you two watch some TV with each other? Maybe it will take your mind off of things," she says.

He holds the phone close to his ear and listens to the voice he has known all his life. He calls his parents and closes his eyes while they talk, his father first, then his mother. Claude is reluctant to hang up. He wants, right now, more than anything, to connect with people who know him from a different part of his life.

•

The next morning Janet wakes up to the sound of typing. Claude is a foot away, at the card table, on his laptop. Janet says hello. He quickly logs off and goes to the kitchen, turning his back on her. She carries her plastic bag of toiletries into the bathroom and locks the door.

Claude goes to work. The day is hot and Janet and Louise spend the entire afternoon inside, watching cars move along the highway. Janet reads a library book aloud. Louise resists anything else.

The next day Janet sits Louise in front of the computer. "This is a time to pamper ourselves," Janet says to Louise. They buy items off an online luxury cosmetics site, something Janet has never done before. Janet does not usually wear makeup. She rarely has manicures or pedicures, and thinks acrylic nails are revolting. She said this once out loud at a dinner party, and the hostess held up her hand, fluttering her fake nails.

When the products arrive they get started right away. The buttery creams smell like frosting and Janet rubs them into the cracks between their fingers and on Louise's forehead and cheeks. She paints Louise's toenails a bright red, putting cotton balls between each toe. She does her own, too, but when she gets up to answer the phone, thinking it will be the doctor with an update, she smudges her polish on the carpet. It is not the doctor. She takes all the color off.

Janet fastens a fresh bra on Louise, moving in a brisk, no-nonsense fashion that signals there is nothing wrong with putting a bra on your daughter. She whistles.

•

I mostly cry in the morning, with Claude, when we wake up and remember. It is unsettling to cry with your partner. There is no one to do the job of comforting.

CHAPTER NINE

S ix days have gone by, and the doctor still has not called. Janet and Claude push Louise's feet into tennis shoes. It is time for her to get out of the apartment. They will take a field trip to the grocery store.

Outside in the brightness, the three of them stare down the three flights of stairs that lead to the parking lot. Louise says no way. Claude stands behind Louise and lifts her by her armpits, and Janet stands in front of her, holding her hands and coaching her down each step. It takes a while. Claude sees a woman open her door, look at their progress, and shut it again. A man waits for them to get all the way down before he runs up the stairs two at a time.

Louise sits in the car while Janet and Claude go in. All Louise wants to eat is potato chips and lemon-lime soda, so that is what they buy.

•

The next day, Louise can walk around the apartment a little. She slides her left arm, the good arm, along the wall. Janet is so proud she has to fight off tears. The right side of Louise's body is drooping a bit. When Louise slips and thuds against the wall, Janet pretends not to see.

One of Janet's friends suggests they take up knitting. Knitting is very soothing, she says, and will distract them while they wait for the doctor to call. Janet drives to a crafts store. She buys needles and wool and a book that will teach them how to make a scarf. Louise is agreeable. Janet reads the steps slowly, and Louise moves the needles this way and that. It is difficult with her right hand. The yarn becomes a tangled mess. Louise drops the needles and hides her face in her lap, squeezing her scalp. Janet puts on a movie. They watch it on mute. Any electronic sound is fuzz, her daughter says.

●

Claude joins an online baseball team. He stays at his office until late into the night to play. He bets money. He accidentally wakes Janet up when he comes back to the apartment. Janet looks at him harshly but says nothing. He brushes his teeth and feels guilty about what Janet must assume. If she asked him point blank, he might admit that cheating had crossed his mind, but no, of course he never would.

Claude and Louise still share a bed, a queen-sized. Louise had chosen a headboard but they had not gotten around to buying it yet. When they first moved in together they'd spent a lot of time at the wholesale store. Their membership card was platinum. They'd stared at the hampers of frozen chicken wings, the aluminum trays of Caesar salad, the barrels of mayonnaise. Who would need all that? they'd said to each other. What kind of people needed so much?

When Claude gets under the covers he feels angry at Louise for being just a body to sleep next to, nothing else, then feels bad for his anger. He tells Louise he loves her, but she must be asleep, because there is no reply.

●

Claude, Janet, and Louise go to Butterfly Beach. They sit on the steps of the stairway that leads to the sand. A floppy orange hat hides Louise's eye patch a little. Claude notices there are many dogs around that their owners can't control. The dogs bite each other's throats and the people tug hard on their leashes. He puts his arm around Louise, as if she might run out there.

Later they drive down the village's main street. They park the car to people watch. A woman raps on Louise's window. It's Danica, a waitress from the Spanish restaurant where Louise used to work nights. Claude's boss lunches there often. He enjoys the fresh flowers and tasteful cleavage.

Claude reaches across Louise and cranks open the window. "We all have a card for you," Danica says. Louise says thank you. "I could swing by and get it sometime," Claude says.

"Or me," says Janet.

The good will between Janet and Claude is going away. Once, when Claude was sitting in his car late at night, Janet knocked on his window, startling him so much he gave a shout. What are you doing? she'd mouthed.

Claude remembers how, when he and Louise first started dating in college, they used to take a break from their copy-editing shift to hit golf balls in the parking lot. Louise would wind up for a big swing and often miss the ball completely. Claude always hit his, precise and quick, and the balls would silently float away. They usually had cigarettes hanging out of their mouths. They never tried to find the balls they hit into the darkness. They never gave those balls a second thought.

Where are you, Louise? he thinks. Are you coming back?

•

Janet thinks Claude's cologne is effeminate. His condiments in the refrigerator are frivolous, his hair products inside the medicine cabinet an embarrassment.

At the end of the week, they get the call from the hospital. The neurosurgeon says he's sorry, but he will not perform the surgery. It is too risky, too much could go wrong. Janet protests. "Then where do we go?" she asks. "I don't know," he says.

CHAPTER TEN

D own the street from Claude and Louise's apartment is an exotic bird shop. A while ago a sign on the door said "Bird Owner's Brunch Today," and Claude thought it would be fun to see what that was all about. Claude used to have a thing for birds. The inside was painted pink and the walls were lined with cages full of small shrieking feathered things. Claude wanted to see the back courtyard, where the wire crates were kept on stilts. Bird owners were mingling out there, walking slowly with their pets on their shoulders and juice in their hands. The birds screamed and nipped at each other. Beaks stuck through honeycombed mesh, pecking anyone who stood too close. Muffins, fruit, and bowls of seeds were displayed, buffet style, on a card table that the birds trampled on. Claude stood in the corner, sunglasses on to protect his eyes, while Louise chatted with the owners, watchful for dangerous ones. There were too many out of their cages, Claude thought. Ladies in expensive knits let the birds climb into their sticky hair, using their ears as steps. Heavy gold earrings swung. A tan man in a Hawaiian shirt told Louise to hold out her arms, and together they made a bridge for his parrot to walk across. It bobbed its head as it walked toward Louise, stuck out its tongue, and tasted the tip of her nose. Louise had stood perfectly still. Claude ran up behind her, ready to swat the bird away, but the parrot leaped at him. It snapped Claude's sunglasses in half.

Louise had laughed about it for the rest of the day, but Claude felt hurt and cheated by those birds. That wasn't how it was supposed to go.

CHAPTER ELEVEN

W arner, Louise's father, knows there is no one to blame. It was just a medical fluke. But still, he wonders if back when she was nine she should have been on a longer bed rest. Should the doctors have done more tests? Maybe the divorce had been stressful. Did Louise stay out late at night? Did she sleep enough? What about alcohol, cigarettes? Warner does not think he is the right sort of father for this situation at all.

•

Warner is an artist, a painter. He does landscapes, working from photographs taken from planes. Crops, rivers, and subdivisions make interesting designs, he thinks. He has taught college classes, but he is happier working in solitude. He wears glasses that are metal and angular, and cooks hot and sour soup from scratch. His cats are on antidepressants. He likes to put on corduroys and mock turtlenecks and ride his bicycle. He used to be a businessman, the publisher of a newspaper. After Louise's first incident, in fourth grade, the two spent a lot of time together in his studio, where he painted at night. They would watch operas he had taped, *The Marriage of Figaro* or *The Magic Flute*. He and Janet separated when Louise was 12 years old. He had moved into a rental house a few miles away, and on the kids' first night over, the potatoes had exploded in the oven and the toilet clogged. Louise had helped him pick out new dishes and bedspreads.

It wasn't that he and Janet fought much, at least not back then. The problem was that Janet liked dinner parties and activities like karate and tennis. She liked the company of other people. Warner had a total of three friends, and even that was too many. After the divorce everything was fine for a while—that is, until Janet decided to take over her father's newspaper in Iola, Kansas. She took the kids with her. Louise had been out of high school, Tom and Michael in grade school. After that they could not speak anymore without saying something vicious.

Janet has called to say they will need to find another surgeon, but in the meantime, she needs to go back to Kansas for a week to manage the paper. Warner leaves his new wife, Elizabeth, at home in Michigan and goes to Santa Barbara to be with his daughter. Warner has not seen his daughter sick in bed like this since she was a child. Actually there was one time, shortly after he and Janet divorced, that he found Louise standing over the sink in her pajamas very early in the morning. She'd just thrown up in the sink. He knew she'd been out late with her friends, but he didn't say anything, and neither had she.

●

Warner is not sure what to do after Janet leaves Louise's apartment. He decides to make Louise a cup of tea. He finds fruity flavors in a drawer and puts one in a cup with water and microwaves it. He peeks inside their bedroom. It is worse than a college dorm. Mattress on the floor. Open suitcases. The walls, bare. Clothes everywhere. And the living room—nothing there but a canvas couch and a small television. Who could heal in a place like this?

Louise tries to sit up when she sees him, but gets tangled in the purple sheets and he has to help her. She is wearing a giant red T-shirt with a stretched-out neckline. Her left eye is drooping and bloodshot. Her lips are chapped and crusted. The last time he'd seen her was Thanksgiving, and

Warner remembers teasing her and Claude as they posed for a picture, saying that they looked like a couple he'd seen in a magazine at the supermarket. Louise had polished off three silver cans of energy juice, but that had been the extent of his worries. He thinks of what he'd just seen on the drive from LAX: endless, bland beaches, showy Italian cars, groups of spoiled women in jogging suits. He'd warned her not to move to Santa Barbara. It's a terminus, he'd said.

Warner pats the covers around Louise, rubbing her arms as if she's cold. Are you hungry? What sounds good? What can I bring you? What can I do?

•

Warner tells Louise he would like to take her to Uncle Charlie's house up in the Santa Ynez Valley, forty-five minutes away. It is quiet there, with golden hills and vineyards, fields of lavender and horses. Unlike here, with the highway so close.

Louise starts crying. He can smell her medicine breath. Claude comes in the apartment handling cigarettes and a fast-food drink. She calls out to him.

They give Louise Xanax and she becomes more agreeable. Claude makes sure she has all the necessary gear. Warner is glad Claude knows about these things, although he wishes Claude would button up his shirt a bit more. Claude gets in the passenger seat and lets Warner drive. He asks Warner questions about his art. Not such a bad guy, Warner thinks. The drive through the canyon winds and winds. Louise faces the window. Warner wonders if she is looking at the scenery, or at her reflection with that eye patch.

They pull up to the house, which is stucco with pillars and rambling. It is ten minutes away from Michael Jackson's Neverland Ranch.

•

As soon as Louise is tucked into bed, Claude says he has to drive back to the office to catch up on work. Warner drinks wine on the patio with Charlie and his sister-in-law. When Louise calls down the hallway, Warner jogs to her bedroom. Her eye patch is off. One eye is crossed. He looks. Louise says she is feeling a bit better, so he carries her outside. She has not moved in many days; her right side is too weak to support her. The night is cool. Small white lights are strung up around some chairs and a fountain trickles. She talks with her aunt and uncle. Warner wonders about his daughter. He has no clue if Louise reads magazines or watches the news. He doesn't know who her friends are, or if they are smart. He can't remember if Janet is a good mother, and if she is, then what exactly she is good at. Warner can't remember teaching Louise anything of importance. He doesn't recall showing his children how to solve a math equation or mow a lawn. He wonders what they think of him. He wonders what he has missed.

The next day, Warner and his brother sit in the kitchen, petting Charlie's two small dogs, golden corgis with big ears. "She's not eating," Warner says. They wonder if the anti-anxiety medication or the headache pills have killed Louise's appetite. They try and think of foods that will tempt her.

"Fast food? Or is she a salad girl?" Charlie asks.

"I don't know," Warner says. "I don't know what she likes."

The brothers look similar. They both have neat hair and are slim. They walk with their hands in their pockets, swaying a little. Charlie plays the piano and wears cashmere sweaters in earthy tones. He has an office in Santa Barbara, but no one can ever remember what it is that he does.

Louise can hear them talking as she lies in the bedroom. She is afraid that she needs to be thought of in this way, as someone whose nutrition and emotional health must be monitored. She feels removed from her body and what is happening to her, and she watches herself like a ghost.

"Meditation?" says Warner.

"Maybe stretching," Charlie suggests.

•

Warner has researched Louise's condition late at night on the internet and found a neurosurgeon in Phoenix who wrote a book called *The Color Atlas of Microneurosurgery.* Apparently, the neurosurgeon listens to heavy metal rock music while he operates. Warner is compiling a list of surgeons to contact. He has four big books on illnesses of the brain and is reading them simultaneously. His brother and sister-in-law help him research. Their teenage children keep Louise entertained with funny movies and teenager talk. The coffee table is now a mailing center, full of envelopes and sticky pads. The only topic of conversation: Louise's health.

Warner feels alone in all of this. It's his own fault, he knows. He should call his wife Elizabeth more often, talk longer. The last time they spoke she'd offered to come to California, and he hadn't really given her a straight answer. In truth he's not sure he could handle any more changes right now.

He thinks about Claude. They have only been together, what, a year? This must be more than he bargained for. Claude usually shows up during the ten o'clock news, and Warner has noticed that when Claude hugs her, she hangs on so tight, for such a long time, that Claude has to shake her off. Warner wonders if it is love, or fear, that makes Louise act the way she does.

Louise will let no one shower her but Claude. She wants Claude to do everything. Claude sets an alarm that goes off every two hours during the night so he can give her those pills. Their bedroom is right below Warner's, and sometimes Warner wakes up and just listens, wondering if he should go knock on the door and see if Louise is awake. But what would he say?

•

Warner and Louise go for daily walks in the backyard, which is full of trees. She can't balance on her own, but she can shuffle, with long pauses between steps, leaning on trees. Warner helps hold her up. Fields of grapes can be seen from a distance, yellow shuttle buses of tourists.

"Remember when we took the trip to Sea World?" Louise asks. "Before Michael was born? And our car broke down on the freeway?"

Warner says yes.

"When you left the car to find a pay phone, I thought you were never coming back," Louise says. "Mom told me not to drink any more juice boxes because Tom needed the last one. I thought she meant that was the last juice box ever, and that you were gone forever, and that we would all die. Dumb, right?" She laughs.

Warner doesn't know what to say. He isn't sure what she's getting at, but it seems important, so he takes her hands off the tree and puts her arms around him, holding her steady.

•

Louise is thinking of another trip. She'd just graduated high school, and Warner surprised her with a trip to Paris, just the two of them. He took her to Versailles and the Louvre. They'd walked up to the Sacré-Cœur Basilica. He'd smoked a cigar while she ate ice cream and looked at the city sparkling below.

On the last afternoon they ate sandwiches in a dark café at a table next to an old man and his Great Dane and discussed the Monica Lewinsky scandal. For some reason her father was defending Clinton. "Dad, he's the president!" she'd said. Louise had been amazed that Warner wasn't more outraged. The blue dress, the cigar, all of it.

Warner swished his wine around, staring into the glass.

"Really, it's not that interesting," he'd said. "As you get

older, you'll find that people do all sorts of idiotic things."
She'd stared at him. She'd been drinking red wine.

"Let's order dessert," he said. "You're young, you should
have something."

Louise had been unsettled by this conversation. She had
wanted there to be certainty. She had wanted her father
to weigh in. But now she thinks she understands what he
meant. Other people's actions and their problems are not of
her concern. We all, sooner or later, have enough drama in
our own lives to keep us occupied. We all have enough pain
of our own.

●

On Valentine's Day Claude brings Louise flowers and
take-out Italian food. Warner gives her a big cane with a red
bow tied on it. They all laugh about the cane, which has a
four-pronged base for extra stability. Rubber grips! The cane
is the winner. Now she won't have to hang on to furniture for
support. Louise hugs her father, hiding her face in his blazer.
It is clear, now, that she is a disabled person. That is how
everyone sees her, and will continue to see her.

●

On his commute to work early the next morning, Claude
hunches over the steering wheel, shirt unbuttoned, windows
down. He is angry. He hates doing this, hates getting up
early and tiptoeing out of the huge house to avoid seeing
anyone. If Louise wakes up while he is combing his hair she
will start to cry, and attending to that will make him late. He
has gotten lax at caring for her. Her aunt and uncle have a
large, glass shower that he can stand in while Louise sits on
a stool. He sudses her hair quickly with loose fingers. He
brushes her hair but she ruins it by lying down while it is
damp, so it has weird waves. Her skin is red and pimply in a
way he has never seen.

He remembers the Ugly Party she threw with her college

roommates. Everyone was supposed to wear the ugliest, most insane clothes they could find. Louise went to a thrift store and bought a black and teal paisley sweater that she wore as a dress, with a wide belt and fishnet tights and high-heeled gold sandals. It was sexy. She had looked good. She'd cheated.

•

While lying in bed in the dark, Claude asks Louise why she thought the cavernous angioma had burst now. Why now, of all times?

"Maybe you were stressed, moving out here?" he says. "You were anxious about finding a job. Remember?"

"So it's my fault?" Louise asks. "I did this to myself? What about all of those parties you took me to? Those dinners with your terrible boss? The drugs. The drinking. We did all that together. Remember?"

"I didn't mean—that came out wrong."

He knows he should apologize. He should reach over and stroke her face, but he can't make himself. She doesn't say anything more.

Everyone at his job asks what happened to his pretty girl-friend. Was it lack of sleep or unclean air? Bad diet?

Claude knows this does not happen because of nothing. Everything has a cause. People hurt themselves, whether they know it or not.

•

The next day, Warner takes Louise for a car ride around the hills of the Santa Ynez Valley. They barely get out of the driveway before she starts screaming. Her eyes do not know where to look, she says. She tears off her eye patch and covers her ears and presses her head to her knees. "The light, it hurts, it hurts," she moans. Warner is scared. She is getting worse, he thinks. He thinks of his own father, who used to taunt Warner's brother for wearing sunglasses, saying,

"What's the matter, Charlie? The sun hurts your precious eyes?" And to Warner, "What's up with the paintbrushes? Why don't you go to military school and toughen up?" Warner would never run a finger across the top of Louise's dresser to see if she had dusted. He would never make her pull weeds in the hot sun while he sat on the porch drinking scotch. He wants Louise to know he is a comforting, sensitive dad. He wants her to know he is sorry for the car ride, for her pain, for not knowing any better than he does.

"This isn't a contest to see who is the bravest," he says. "You can always tell me what you want. Would you like to go inside and sit on the couch? Do you want your eye pillow, the one filled with lavender buds? How about that? Some soda?"

"Dad," Louise cries. "Soda is not what I want."

●

Claude picks Louise up from Uncle Charlie's and takes her back to their Santa Barbara apartment. She has a flight the next morning to go back to Kansas to be with her mother for a while, until the family can find another surgeon.

Claude packs up her things. "Your mom can help you better than we can."

She watches him. "I don't want to go."

By the time Claude is finished packing her up it is dark out. He says he is going to the office. She begins to cry.

"Look," he says, "I took the afternoon off to drive you here so you can lie under a blanket, just like you would do anywhere."

"Don't you want to spend our last night together?" she asks.

"It's not like it's our last night ever."

"But what if it is?"

Claude runs out to Louise's favorite take-out place. He waits in a long line and finally leaves with the seafood soup and corn tortillas she says she can't live without. Claude likes the way things are going at work. His boss tells him he is smart and has potential, even stops by Claude's desk sometimes to chat about the national news or sports. He assigned Claude an interview with the golf club president and printed the whole thing verbatim on the front page with Claude's byline. Claude makes sure to never leave work before his boss, and he is always serious, unless, of course, he needs to laugh at a joke, or make one. He can't ditch his job now. He knows that's what she wants.

When Claude gets back to the apartment Louise is watching a crime show. She begs him to please not leave her alone. "If a serial killer breaks in, how would I defend myself?"

Claude sees she is serious. He starts yelling. He gets close to her neck, saying she is a bloodsucker, that he is no nurse. Why doesn't she try to help herself? Why doesn't she do something to improve her situation instead of just lying around? She throws her shoe at him. He slams the door.

The office is empty. He sits in his boss's leather chair. The phone rings and rings, but he does not answer. He switches on the computer. He stays there all night.

CHAPTER TWELVE

Warner and Janet email.

The emails begin with "Hi" and "Dear." They end with "Best."

One thing about the trouble with their daughter: It has made them want to be kind.

CHAPTER THIRTEEN

The main industry in Janet's town, Iola, Kansas, is a chocolate candy factory. There is also a defunct rubber plant.

When Janet sees Louise helped off the plane by an attendant she is shocked. Her daughter is still wearing an eye patch. She has a cane, and her limp is worse. Her T-shirt and sweatpants look like she's been wearing them for a week. Louise is crabby and teary and can't even snap her right fingers together anymore.

Janet feels guilty. Her shirt is crisp and clean. Her hair is curled under and held back with a headband. She does a yoga video every day and has an exercise ball. She rarely gets sick. Louise has very little luggage. Janet grips her daughter's arm and leads her to the car.

People around town have filled Janet's house with gifts for Louise: a stuffed toy lamb, a framed poem about Jesus, a sign to hang over a doorknob about staying strong. Janet has opened piles of cards, most of which contain pre-printed phrases such as, "We are praying for you," "Everything happens for a reason," or "God has a plan." Louise had announced that she does not believe in God and is irritated by people who do. Janet goes to church, but seeing Louise like this, she has to wonder.

Louise walks past all the gifts and turns on the TV.

•

Claude calls Louise, but not as often as he should. She can't hear that well. He keeps having to repeat: "I miss you. I love you. How are you feeling?" Louise says Claude should send her more letters and packages, that he should buy one of those video cameras he can hook up to his computer, that he should always answer his cell phone when she calls, no matter what. She reminds him of the sweet things he used to do for her, like the time in college when she flew out to visit him, and he blindfolded her outside his house, a white duplex on a little street, saying he had a surprise. It had been night, and the air had smelled like a candle. You could hear the ocean and the neighborhood was quiet. He took her by the hand and led her up the stairs, carefully, so she would not fall. There was a trail of rose petals leading to the bedroom. All the lights were off and little votive candles made a heart shape on the floor. A bubble bath was filling up. "It had been like a dream," she says to Claude now. "It had been what every girl wanted."

He wonders how she had been seduced by such a romantic cliché. He had seen the whole routine in a movie once and done it for other girls before Louise. He wonders if she's lost all her irony.

Claude hangs up feeling tired and hungry. Louise sends him a long email that he can hardly read, huge blocks of rageful text with almost every word misspelled—the result of her typing with one hand, and the drowsing effects of the medication, he guesses.

•

The Montecito planning commission is beginning to like him. Its sleek members invite him to play tennis and go on fundraising beach walks. A woman named J'Ayme (i.e., "Jamie") Brenner, a realtor of beachfront houses for celebrities, asks him to brunch one Sunday. The place usually has an hour-long wait, but of course not for her. Over fruit, coffee, and smoked salmon, J'Ayme tells Claude about a star who is moving to the area and planting an organic herb garden.

"Perfect story material, and you're the only one who knows!" J'Ayme winks. "I'll give you all my exclusives." She leans across the table and asks Claude if she has something in one of her eyes. Her breasts hover over the salmon.

The apartment is now Claude's. He smokes inside, and leaves spilled corn chips on the floor. He plans to invite some guys from the office over soon to watch a basketball game. They'll have beers, order a pizza.

Claude goes to Butterfly Beach to write a story on a cancer benefit. Its mascot is a teddy bear. He is surrounded by women in bathing suits with metal belts and leather fringe. A woman in sunglasses and a white one-piece talks to him about the foundation. There is a large hole in the fabric that exposes her stomach. Claude nods and writes in his notebook. Trays of free drinks, called Teddy-tinis, are being passed around by sweaty waiters in tuxedos.

"Cancer does not stop in a financial downturn," the woman says to Claude.

Claude thinks about touching her stomach. Her skin would be warm.

CHAPTER FOURTEEN

When I step outside to pick up a package on the front porch I think of what I must look like to the people who live on my mother's street. My face is faded. My pink sweatpants are stained with cereal bits and coffee spills. I seldom wear a bra. I think about what would happen if Claude saw me like this. We would both be ashamed. I want him to be here but at the same time I do not. I don't know what we would do. I don't go on walks here like I did with my father in California. Iola is small and the houses are close together. It's not like Santa Barbara with the boutiques and gardens and eucalyptus trees. No one walks anywhere unless they have a destination.

The floor in my mother's house is waxed oak. It is filled with heavy dark furniture that once belonged to my grandparents, and my mattress rests in a giant, carved maple frame. My arms and legs are shrinking from lack of use. They are all bruised, and the bruises look like fingerprints. My hip bones are purple from doorways and corners.

While my mother is at work, I sit in the computer room upstairs. There is only a small desk, walls of books, and a roller chair that gets stuck in the carpet. For the first time, I do a Google search of "cavernous angioma." What comes up scares me. On message boards, mothers write sad posts about children who have died from what I have, or who have severe brain damage from the craniotomy it takes to remove it. The Angioma Alliance puts on conferences all over the country. I imagine my family attending one, seeing hundreds of people who look just as dreary and wadded up as we do.

At my mother's I watch a lot of TV. *The O.C.* and *Laguna Beach*. Anything about wealthy teenagers in California with boyfriend problems. My mother thinks I'm torturing myself, but watching beautiful people with petty problems helps me feel superior, somehow.

I find a stack of photo albums in the computer room and cannot resist looking through them. I hardly recognize that girl with a beer in her hand wearing a peacoat on a snowy balcony, or that one, dancing in a bright blue dress with a boy whose hands clutch her satin behind. So many pictures of me in Italy standing alone in front of some statue, some church, some ruins, grinning at nothing.

I had grown up in the typical way and had typical photos to prove it, but they were not promises for a typical life.

LOUISE KRUG

CHAPTER FIFTEEN

It is early spring, and the big, empty sky is gray. There are no hills, and small black dots are cows. At the grocery store, real farmers with overalls and hats buy food just like everybody else.

Janet washes Louise's clothes: pajama pants and old T-shirts from Tom and Michael's drawers. Michael, in his senior year of high school now, is hardly ever around. He brought a friend over a few weeks ago, and Louise had stayed in her room the whole night, shouting at Janet when she knocked on the door. Tom is away at college, a two-hour drive away. He says he will visit soon. Janet's boyfriend lives even farther, and has a new grandbaby. So mostly it is just Janet and Louise.

Janet stacks the dishes in the dishwasher. There is not much else for her to do.

•

Janet decides: Enough of this. She takes Louise to a physical therapist. No one has told her to do this, but it seems logical enough. Louise can tolerate being in a car now. The gym is a white, cinderblock building off the town's main street. Weights, blocks, and bands sit in bins. The physical therapist looks like a college kid, but he says he is married with three children. Janet explains Louise's situation, and the physical therapist says maybe he can help.

He has Louise step up a set of wooden stairs built into

the wall, then down. He has her curl weights, touch her toes, do squats against the wall. Janet is hopeful. She has always had confidence in athletics and sweat. She used to run half marathons and do aerobics, and now works out on the elliptical machine in her basement every day after work. She always pushed her children to do sports growing up because she thought it would make them grow into fit, disciplined adults. She didn't want them to be lazy.

The physical therapist stands a few feet away and watches a baseball game on TV.

When the session is over the physical therapist gives them a laminated packet of illustrated exercises. The first three are noted to especially help patients with a rotator cuff injury. Janet and Louise look at one another. A rotator cuff injury?

In the parking lot, a group of boys in basketball shorts glance at Louise, then quickly look away. There was a time when boys like that would have made something out of Louise.

They don't bother going back.

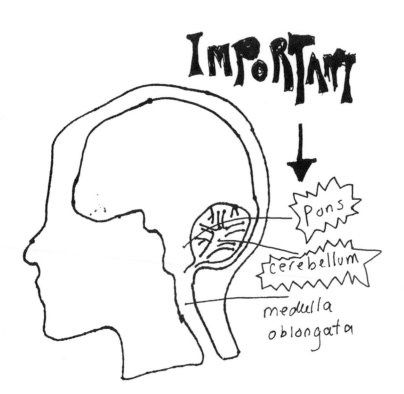

200 First Street SW
Rochester, Minnesota 55905
████████████████

Fredric B. Meyer, M.D.
Department of Neurologic Surgery

April 25, 2005

RE: Ms. Louise L. Stauffer

Ms. Louise L. Stauffer
PO Box 151
Summerland, CA 93067-0151

████████████████

Dear Ms. Stauffer:

Thank you very much for your kind note. It was a great honor and pleasure for me and the entire team to have the opportunity to care for you.

I hope that your recovery will continue to go well and that ultimately you will have excellent neurological function. As we have discussed, this may take some time, up to a year. However, it is my sincere hope that your recovery will be complete.

Most importantly, I think that you are a brave and impressive woman. Few would have had the fortitude and courage to face high risk surgery as you did. You were inspiring to all of us!

Please keep me informed of your progress over time.

With warmest personal wishes and best regards,

Respectfully yours,

Fredric B. Meyer, M.D.
Professor and Chair

FBM:mjw

Clinical Document Copy

PM&R Brain Rehab Hospital Service
Dismissal Summary

20-Apr-2005

Ms. Louise L. Stauffer

Printed: 20-Apr-2005 12:01 by User ID: 14106302

Page 1 of 8

DEMOGRAPHIC INFORMATION:

Patient Name: Ms. Louise L. Stauffer
Age: 22 Y
Note Date: 20-Apr-2005
Saint Marys Hospital - Hospital Summary
Admission Date: 5-Apr-2005 Dismissal Date: 20-Apr-2005
Dismissing Consultant: Allen W. Brown, MD
Mayo Clinic 24-hour coverage telephone#: (507) 284-2511

Address: PO Box 151 City: Summerland, CA 93067-0151
History Section: HSEN # 2 Service: PMRBI Type/Desc: SUM Status: TrxF Revision #: 15

ADVANCE DIRECTIVES:
Patient has advanced directives.

CODE STATUS:
Resuscitate

SUMMARY DIAGNOSES:
#1 Pontine cavernous hemangioma s/p hemorrhage and resection 3/30/05; 4/1/05.
#2 Spastic right hemiparesis with atexia.
#3 Truncal ataxia.
#4 Peripheral left facial weakness
#5 Lagophthalmos, status-post lateral blepharorrhaphy.
#6 Intranuclear ophthalmoplegia
#7 Multiple bilateral extraocular cranial nerve nuclei impairments.
#8 Post-operative urinary retention, resolved.
#9 Steroid psychosis, resolved.

CHIEF COMPLAINT/REASON FOR ADMISSION:
Cavernous hemangioma s/p resection

ADMISSION PROBLEMS:
Ms. Stauffer is a pleasant, 22-year-old left-handed journalist from California with a past medical history of a known pontine cavernous hemangioma s/p hemorrhage x 3 who presented to Mayo Clinic for further evaluation and treatment options following repeat hemorrhage and neurologic deficit February 1, 2005.

Ms. Stauffer's neurologic difficulties began at the age of eight when she was in the fourth grade when she experienced the acute onset of headache, right-sided weakness, and diplopia. She had a CT and MRI which reportedly showed a "brain stem cavernous angioma". At that time, she was hospitalized at the University of Michigan, and the recommendation was to observe. She spontaneously improved completely back to normal within six weeks. She did well until high school, when she had two repeat episodes both associated with diplopia and headache with rapid recovery and no residua.

Then, on February 1, 2005, while working at a restaurant, she experienced the fairly abrupt onset of a holocephalic headache which progressed in severity over several hours. Shortly thereafter, she noted the onset of tingling and clumsiness of her right hand which came on while she was sitting and watching a movie. Her headache was worse at that time as well, and she went to an emergency room in Santa Barbara where she had a CT and then MRI which showed what she describes as a "two centimeter bleed" in the brain stem. She was evaluated by neurosurgery there

MB3C&F APPOINTMENT CARD

Name Louise Stauffer

Room No. 54B

Date 4/7

Morning	Afternoon
7:	1:00
8:00 ADL	1:45 PT
8:	2:00
9:00	2:
9:	3:00
10:00 PT	3:30 OT
10:	4:00
11:00 OT	4:
11:	

(SPT) Speech Therapy	(PSY) Psychology
(PT) Physical Therapy	(PSI) Psychometric Testing
(OT) Occupational Therapy	(ADL) Activities of Daily Living
(RT) Recreational Therapy	(SG) Support Group
(SW) Social Worker	(OG) Orientation Group
	(PCC) Patient Care Conference

MB3C/F APPOINTMENT CARD

Name: Louise Stauffer

Room # 54B

Date: 4/20

Morning	Afternoon
7:00 ADL	1:00
8:00	1:30 PT
8:	2:00
9:00	2:
9:45 PT	3:00 OT
10:00	3:
10:	4:00
11:00 OT	4:
11:	

(SPT) Speech Therapy	(PSY) Psychology
(PT) Physical Therapy	(PSI) Psychometric Testing
(OT) Occupational Therapy	(ADL) Activities of Daily Living
(RT) Recreational Therapy	(SG) Support Group
(SW) Social Worker	(OG) Orientation Group
	(PCC) Patient Care Conference

Typical days at
in-patient rehab

Rehabilitation Progress Report

Louise Stauffer

Estimated Discharge Date:	4/20/2005

Team Conference Date:	4/13/2005

Discharge to: Father's House

Areas to focus on next week:

Improve balance

Increase walking quality and distances

Arm and leg strengthening

Transfer training

Increase independence with dressing and toileting

Identify equipment for home

Provide recreational therapy resources near home area

Provide room-based materials (books, music, videos)

16PF® Fifth Edition
Personal Career Development
Profile *Plus* (PCDP+)

Name: Louise L. Stauffer
Date: April 30, 2005

This report describes Ms. Stauffer's typical personal lifestyle patterns.
The narrative in her report is based on her scores from the 16PF Fifth
Edition Questionnaire and additional predictive research.

The PCDP is founded on 35 years of research and consulting experience
of organizational and management professionals. This experience
revealed that people who are effectively directing the course and growth
of their careers reflect personal strengths anchored to five important areas
of behavior covered in this report:

- Problem-Solving Resources
- Patterns for Coping with Stressful Conditions
- Interpersonal Interaction Styles
- Organizational Role and Work-Setting Preferences
- Career Activity Interests

The purpose of this report is to help Ms. Stauffer broaden her
understanding of herself and to plan well for her future. Although
successful people possess personal strengths inherent to these behavioral
patterns, no lifestyle can be classified as "the best way of doing things."
Various styles may aid in one's efforts to be successful, happy, and
productive.

A helpful understanding of Ms. Stauffer's reported personal strengths
should also take into account other significant information about her, such
as her work and leisure experiences, education and skills. So, if Ms.
Stauffer wants to benefit fully from this report, she should discuss her
profile with a skilled counselor or trained professional. **Of utmost
importance, though, this report should be treated confidentially and
responsibly.**

Ms. Stauffer would most likely function with greater personal effectiveness, both on-the-job and in other personal-career situations, if she would try to be aware of and work consciously to guard against the impact of:

- her tendency, at times, to act with such a positive outlook that she may fail to prepare herself enough for what she undertakes;
- reacting to some situations with such enthusiasm and spontaneity that possible consequences of what she does may not be sufficiently anticipated or considered;
- the tendency to make spur-of-the-moment decisions, rather than giving enough thoughtful consideration of future consequences of such actions;
- the tendency to enjoy risk-taking and being involved in adventurous activities, especially when a more cautious approach could be taken to what is being done;
- tendencies to become overly impatient when confronted with what she may view as possible roadblocks to doing things valued by her as being important;
- being overly confident about her ability to handle most any problem or situation that comes up, when more accurate thinking and more realistic planning may be required to accomplish what she most desires to do;
- taking on assignments in such an expedient way that she could overlook critically important details that require thoughtful deliberation and planning;
- being so overly confident about trying new approaches to some problems and situations that the benefits of first exploring what others may have to contribute to the solutions sought may be overlooked;
- being so open and spontaneous with most people when it may be more effective if she were more discreet or would play her cards closer to her chest;
- the effect of showing too little interest in living up to the standards that society values, or simply doing what she thinks is expected of her by other people;
- making more of an effort to avoid conforming to policies and rules established by others than trying to productively follow or work within them;
- tendencies to be less prepared and organized than she could strive to be because she may not be aware of her need to build more effective work habits than she seems to have at this time;
- urges to change from one career field or job to another, or to not stay with one organization long enough to feel as if she belongs there;

and in addition,

- taking on activities or tasks that take time and effort to work on theoretical issues and problems, since Ms. Stauffer's strengths seem to indicate that she is much more effective doing more practical tasks. Even so, she appears to be able to work creatively on practical tasks so as to bring innovations to what she does or thinks is important.

In conclusion, Ms. Stauffer is usually happy and willing to simply be herself in most situations.

These directions are intended for home treatment and not as a prescription for use by a professional physical therapist. Perform _____ repetitions of each exercise _____ times daily, as indicated by your therapist.

9. Draw the point of the nose downward, narrowing the nostrils.

10. Draw the corner of the mouth straight upward, deepening the furrow from the side of the nose to the side of the mouth.

11. Raise and protrude the upper lip.

12. Close the lips and protrude them forward.

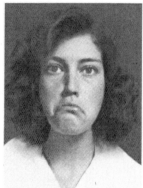

13. Press the cheeks firmly against the teeth, pulling back the corners of the mouth. (Draw the chin backward.)

14. Draw the corners of the mouth downward.

15. Draw the lower lip and corners of the mouth downward and outward, tensing the skin over the neck.

16. Protrude the jaw on each side.

Notes

5x's

1. Pucker & Relax

2. Smile & FROWN

3. Tongue Cheek to Cheek

4. Straw side to side.

Count the number of times the double numbers appear in each row and write it on the line on the right side of the page 3M

88 9567884650338868668894388 ____

33 3357684923385692337673833 ____

44 4574488274423466473284456 ____

22 7856322742290642456224652 ____

66 6758493668594866886683645 ____

55 4625655346558956557837556 ____

99 8990934633896993437283996 ____

11 9171741147563211678534117 ____

77 3477117123767756472340976 ____

99 9287499234728969932199120 ____

22 3432278756232782274822392 ____

Check your work: 4, 4, 3, 3, 3, 4, 3, 3, 2, 3, 3

Warren, M. (1996). Prereading and writing exercises for persons with macular scotomas. Birmingham AL:
© 1996 visABILITIES Rehab Services Inc.

•SHOPPING CENTERS/MALL/ STORES

MOVIES/SHOPPING/SPECIAL EVENTS

EXERCISE

USABLE OPTIONS (MOBILITY/SERVICE)

•UNITED WAY/SERVICE ORGANIZATIONS

VOLUNTEERISM

ASSISTANCE

Ms. Louise Stauffer
Time Management/Recreational Planning sheet

The idea and input below is to provide a general outline of resources, ideas, new and old interests and consider the therapeutic value in six domains: Social interaction, Physical exercise, Spectator appreciation, Intellectual stimulation, Creative expression and Solitary relaxation. Please refer to the dotted items and folder for information that has been compiled. All areas should be considered on the 5 W's (Who, What, When, Where, Why and How) plus the consideration of supervision and safety/risk involved. All areas need to consider time, transportation and cost as well how opportunities fit into daily life schedule. Moderation and return to activities should be gradual based on endurance, enjoyment and tolerance of Ms. Stauffer. **Remember** this list is not all inclusive but acts as a guide to be added or reduced as needed

- Please refer to file on Grand Valley State university contact, water aerobic self plan, Recreation is where you find it sheet, and Community resource sheets, and multiple activity list. ▮▮▮▮

- Physical-beach, water aerobics class, stretches for home, walking program each day, pilates tape, free/machine weights.

- Intellectual Stimulation-word finds, crosswords, TV(jeopardy, wheel-o-fortune, Price is Right, board/computer games(solitaire, free cell, majong, etc.), computer skills for e-mail, internet, journaling, and writing skills requiring keyboarding, larger piece puzzles 1-300pc., any billing or checkbook issues, etc.

- Spectator Appreciation-VCR and movie theatre, any sporting events, Theatre/concert opportunities, Listen to music players for types of music (jazz, blues, rock, etc.), people watch at beach/mall/or areas of interest, nature appreciation, etc.

- Social interaction-time with friends and family, community re-integration (order food, current events, topics of interest, etc.)

200 First Street SW
Rochester, Minnesota 55905
████████

Allen W. Brown, M.D.
Physical Medicine and Rehabilitation

September 27, 2005

RE: Ms. Louise L. Stauffer

Ms. Louise L. Stauffer
607 Lawndale Court
Holland, MI 49423-4755
████████████

Dear Ms. Stauffer:

Thanks for updating your progress and your kind words. I am glad that things are generally going well, due largely to your hard work and determination. Institutional policy does not allow me to communicate about patient care through an insecure mode such as e-mail. Other than electrical stimulation and willful activation of the weak facial muscles, there is really no other treatment that has been shown to be effective for this kind of (peripheral nerve) weakness. There may be other things that can be done if it has still not improved in a year or so, but for now I think you should stay with your current approach.

Please stay in touch, and we will see you again when you return to see Dr. Fredric Meyer in 2006.

Sincerely,

Allen W. Brown, M.D.

AWB:ejb

CHAPTER SIXTEEN

C laude gets invited to a party at J'Ayme Brenner's house. The celebrity realtor says she has more gossip that could turn into news for Claude. The house is a wood-shingle mansion with an infinity pool. The kitchen is a rich person's idea of a pioneer cabin. J'Ayme makes Claude a plate of cheese and olives and watches him eat it. His boss is out by the pool, surrounded by leggy women who are all laughing. A man in white linen comes up and shakes Claude's hand, saying he liked Claude's article on the new iced-coffee cart downtown. J'Ayme nudges him.

Claude is feeling pretty good.

He guesses J'Ayme is in her late forties. She dresses much younger. Her hair is long and tiger-striped. Her nails, coppery. Shoes too.

J'Ayme asks him about Louise. Claude tells her everything, he can't help himself. They go to her computer, and Claude shows J'Ayme some of Louise's craziest emails. There are too many to read. He replays some of Louise's voicemails, and J'Ayme's eyebrows raise at the swearing and crying. He tells himself it is okay to share his frustrations with someone. It's not like Louise is keeping her complaints to herself.

He turns circles in J'Ayme's computer chair. "I'm no hero. I'm helping her as much as I can."

"Sounds like she wants you to have no life because hers is gone, too," J'Ayme says.

"Well, I wouldn't say *it's gone*—" Claude says. "I just don't want to feel like the bad guy anymore."

J'Ayme stands behind Claude with her hands on his shoulders. "You have to look out for yourself," she says.

Claude thinks about kissing J'Ayme. He knows that he could. But he wants to continue feeling like someone doing the right thing. He wants to keep conducting himself in a way that is superior to Louise. She could be handling things a little better, he thinks.

J'Ayme wheels him around to face her.

CHAPTER SEVENTEEN

J anet gets tired of explaining to people what "cavernous angioma" means. People come at her from nowhere, asking questions, breathing on her in narrow office hallways and at the grocery store, where she is aching from cold in the dairy section, just wanting a jug of milk. When she is in a hurry, she calls it a stroke. This is not a lie, exactly. Both conditions involve the brain, blood, damage, and doctors. Other times at church potlucks she says that Louise has a blood clot that's getting bigger and has to be removed. People know what a blood clot is because the elderly get them all the time, especially in their legs. Occasionally someone will ask if Louise has had an aneurysm, which is just about impossible because those are typically deadly, but Janet will just say yes, an aneurysm, that's right.

Other mothers complain about their in-laws. They show off pictures of their grandchildren. Janet cannot imagine when she will be able to do that.

CHAPTER EIGHTEEN

Someone in Janet's book club is having a makeup party. The woman says it's the kind of makeup you can't buy in drug or department stores—you need a representative with a sticker on her car. As the woman speaks, Janet stares at her spiky-stiff hair and jingly charm bracelets. Still, Janet thinks. Socializing will be good for Louise.

Janet drives the two of them to the woman's house with a wax-papered plate of cookies balanced on her knees. The plate keeps sliding off and bumping the gear shift, but she is afraid to ask Louise to hold them. Louise gets annoyed at everything these days. Her vision is still doubled. Her right hand is unusable and she still has trouble walking without her cane.

"Isn't it fun, being a girl?" Janet asks Louise.

Louise looks the other way.

The kitchen is full of brownies and women. The representative and her daughter, both in sparkly blusher and eye shadow, sit at the head of the table. The daughter is around Louise's age, and has dyed black hair that flips at the sides. She sips a can of Diet Coke through a straw. The daughter says she and her husband are trying to get pregnant. They want a little girl. She asks Janet and Louise to pray for them.

Some ladies gather around Louise and ask about the job she had in California, the one she was supposed to start the day she went to the ER.

"Well, everything happens for a reason," one of the

ladies says, and the rest of them nod their heads in agree-
ment. "God has a plan. You know, plenty of places need good
writers. Even factories need someone to make sure their labels
read like they should!" another says.

"I'm going back to California," Louise says. "My boyfriend's there. He's a journalist, too."

Janet turns away. She doesn't need to see their expressions to know what they are thinking: What would a girl like
Louise do out in California now?

•

The women have removed their makeup and now look
like they have woken up in the middle of the night. At each
place setting is a small bag filled with products and a hand
mirror. The women are told to apply Shimmer Glimmer to
their faces. Janet sees Louise clumsily slap the stuff on, too
much, so her face looks slippery. She won't look in the little
compact mirror. She's just smearing the stuff on her face.

Next comes hair, and this requires individual counseling.
The mother and daughter team go from woman to woman,
talking strategy. They get to Louise and say, "May I?" and
pull out her ponytail, unsnagging the hair from the elastic band of the eye patch. The daughter fluffs and flutters
Louise's hair so the elastic band is hidden. Her fake nails
click.

Janet remembers getting a phone call from Louise when
she first moved to California. Louise had been sitting under
the dryer at Lazlo's Salon and Spa, where she was getting
her hair done by Lazlo himself. Louise told her that Lazlo's
clients were all rich and famous, but that Claude had a con-
nection from his newspaper gig. That day Louise received
a full set of foils, a deep conditioning treatment, and a sexy
shag cut. She'd been there three hours and they still weren't
done! Janet had shaken her head at the time, thinking her
daughter a bit frivolous.

Janet wonders now if she hadn't been a little jealous.

CHAPTER NINETEEN

A t night, Claude plays tennis by himself against a wall at the Coral Club—he is a complimentary member now, thanks to a story he wrote on the club's thriving business. He thinks about his phone call with Louise earlier. She said she'd found a surgeon, a famous neurosurgeon at the Mayo Clinic in Minnesota. Claude had let her talk and talk. The time difference meant that he, in California, was three hours earlier than she. Louise had already watched her fill of TV for the day, eaten, and was now in bed. He was still full of energy.

Claude had told her, softly, that he didn't think he should come. "I won't be any help, baby. I'll lose my job. You'll be back here before we know it." Louise had hung up on him. He called her back and she'd called him horrible names. He'd mostly stayed silent. He's used to her being miserable now. In fact, he can't really remember her ever being in a good mood. Even the night of the premiere, the night her foot first went numb, they'd been fighting in the car. He'd been late to pick her up, and she'd slammed the car door on the way in. She had a toothpaste stain on her shirt. She had been frowning.

He knows that if he goes to the clinic and sits in chairs with Janet and the rest of Louise's family, if he shares a hotel room with her bearded brother, Tom, and teenage Michael, if he eats hospital food in a booth with Warner and Elizabeth, that he will be a good boyfriend in their eyes.

They'll assume he's in it for the long haul. He imagines himself sitting by her bed for months. He imagines her crossed eye. None of this is going away soon.

●

Claude's parents met in France at a dinner party and got married soon after. "Still very much in love," they say frequently and without prompting. Claude's parents now live in Atlanta. He and Louise had spent Christmas with them, and their house had been heavily scented with pink sweeping curtains and a white carpet. His father had cooked king crab. They picked the meat out of the claws with small, gold forks, and dipped the chunks into pots of butter. His mother, a beautiful French woman with black hair, had only eaten crackers. She hadn't said much.

Claude had once told Louise, after drinking too many strawberry margaritas, that he thought his father had cheated. He wasn't a hundred percent, and it was years ago, when his father was traveling to Germany a lot for work. Claude said there was no way his mother knew; if something like that ever happened she'd leave his father forever. Claude always regretted telling Louise this because he sensed it made Louise think less of his father, and maybe less of him.

●

Claude thinks of J'Ayme. Thank god that didn't happen, he thinks, and thwacks the ball as hard as he can.

PART TWO:
THE SURGERIES

CHAPTER TWENTY

T hings in the brain move around like prizes in a Jell-O salad. This is the analogy that the surgeon gives Janet, Warner, Elizabeth, Louise, Tom, and Michael as he explains the difficulties of the upcoming operation. It is the day before the surgery, and they are all crammed in an examination room at the Mayo Clinic in Minnesota. The surgeon draws diagrams on a notepad that illustrate how he is planning on entering the base of Louise's skull. He circles an area. "Here is the prize," the surgeon says. Louise is cheerfully watching the surgeon scribble. She is wearing her eye patch and holding her cane. Janet watches her.

Everyone but Janet oohs and aahs and narrows their eyes in concentration as the surgeon speaks. Janet cannot engage. She cannot think of her daughter's brain as Jell-O salad, which belongs in the grocery store next to the hummus and cheese. It is rainbow colored and comes in a clear plastic mold. It's the fruit-flavored stuff at picnics that nobody eats. Janet never made it for her children. She made cookies sometimes, and brown birthday cakes. She made crisps and cobblers.

Janet doesn't like the idea of food prizes, either. She has heard of marriage proposals that happen at restaurants where the ring is in the center of a crème brûlée, or at the bottom of a bubbling champagne glass. But Janet always thinks of what could go wrong in situations like that. The ring could break someone's tooth, or be swallowed. If the woman finds the ring in her dessert it will be covered with sticky goo. It will have to be rinsed off and cleaned before it is put on the finger. Janet cannot see the fun in that.

•

Janet is getting tired of hearing from the doctors that Louise's cavernous angioma is in the worst possible place it could be, in the pons, which is attached to the brain stem. This is not helpful, she thinks. They are already scared enough. They already walk around the hallways in a daze, confused by doctors who carry sandwiches in plastic baggies and doors that open into gilded chapels. Too many times Janet has gotten off the elevator looking for an ATM and ended up in an unlabeled corridor, clueless about how she got there or how to get back. The cavernous angioma is causing them to buy things like travel pillows so they can sleep in chairs. It has brought them here, to a world-famous clinic with a brain surgeon who says he will try to get it out of Louise's brain so that no one will ever have to worry about it bleeding again.

•

Claude is not here, and Janet hates Claude for this. Her own boyfriend isn't here and she hates him, too. She broke up with him after he told her he couldn't come, right there in the hospital lounge. There had been no unkind words or crying. She feels like she is able to do things now, easily, cleanly, and induce no pain on herself whatsoever. She is like a janitor at the clinic who sweeps up a pile of dirt and tosses it into the garbage. It had taken place in a matter of seconds.

•

The morning of the surgery, Janet, Louise, and the rest of the family get up when it is still dark and walk across the street from the hotel to the clinic. It is a commanding place, a huge block of red brick. They carry water bottles and books. Louise uses her cane.

Janet had spent a lot of time in the hotel bathroom that morning, staring at the mini soaps and shampoos in the shower. She thought about how Louise had been getting better, able to bathe without help, bracing herself against the sides of the stall. Louise will be in bad shape for a while after the operation. The surgeon has told them this. There are no guarantees that the operation will work at all. For instance, removing the cavernous angioma might damage the neurons that control the function of swallowing. That would mean that she would have to be fed through a tube. Forever. And if the nerve connectors are damaged, she will have to be hooked up to a machine that will push the breath in and out. It will be plugged into an electrical outlet. She will have to stay in a bed, or a chair, connected by a cord that comes out of a wall. It won't be like now, how she can go up and down stairs. How she can hold a knife to cut cheese. How she can shake crackers out of a bag.

The surgeon assures them that all of this is unlikely. It is almost certain that swallowing will not be a problem, his assistants say. Or breathing. They say the operation will be worth it.

•

It takes three elevators to get to the small, steel room where a woman has them sign life and death papers. Should something go horribly wrong, who would decide whether or not to keep the patient alive? Louise just sits there.

Janet helps Louise into a hospital gown. They forgot to bring an extra bag, so Janet stuffs Louise's regular clothes into her purse. Janet covers Louise's feet with nonskid socks. She helps Louise into a hairnet. Louise says nothing, does nothing, lets Janet do it all.

In pre-op, the nurse leads Louise to a gurney and helps her lie down. The room is large and white and Janet stands close by. Louise stares at the ceiling squares, eyes wide. There are many others lying here, too, probably fifty of them with blankets covering their legs, waiting to be wheeled off to surgery. Nurses quietly ask questions and consult clipboards. The surgeon comes by. He has on red fleece socks and leather sandals that buckle. A mask covers his mouth. He writes on Louise's forehead with a Sharpie: craniotomy.

When he leaves, Janet bends over and hugs her daughter. She kisses the word, covers it with her cheek.

•

The surgeon and his assistants shave a back strip of Louise's head and use a saw to open a bone flap in Louise's skull. This is a "suboccipital craniotomy." They want to find the cavernous angioma and cut it out, and then they want to seal the veins together again so there is no more bleeding. But they can't find it. They take a tiny camera inside and see only healthy brain. All they see is Jell-O. No prize.

They sew her head back up. They will have to wait another day before they can go back in again.

CHAPTER TWENTY-ONE

Warner has brought a stack of books to read but opens none. Instead, he walks laps around the hospital. The place is huge. If he adds a visit to the library and ducks outside to get some air, he can spend a good hour in motion, which is better than staying still.

Tom is trying to keep Janet from crying. He gets her paper cups of water and makes her come with him to the cafeteria, where they move through a hot-food line like grade-school kids. He tells her stories about his friends at school. He tries to make her laugh. Then he feels awful when her smile turns.

Michael keeps everyone supplied with coffee. He explores. He walks wings with nothing but patient rooms containing somebody lying in the bed like they have been there a very long time. The little TV, suspended in the corner, always blares. Those people will never leave, he thinks.

Elizabeth keeps trying to talk to Warner. He's pacing, distant, hard to reach. She wants to find out what he is thinking. She tries to comfort him, and he looks at her like he doesn't know who she is.

In California, Claude is sure that the surgery will go fine. No one has called him, which he takes as a good sign. He is glad that something is finally getting done.

•

Janet works on a needlepoint pillow cover during the two days in the waiting room. When she is finished she throws it away.

CHAPTER TWENTY-TWO

The next day is April 1. A tornado passes through the town where the clinic is. Shingles come off roofs, wild branches whirl in streets. All of the operating rooms are in the basement, so the surgery continues. This time, the surgeon and his assistants cut open a different section of Louise's skull, a bit higher, but still in the suboccipital part, and there they see the cavernous angioma, oozing. They remove the dark ball of tangled veins and save it to show to the family, as if for proof. They sew and staple her skull back together and wrap it tight. They unscrew her head from the vise that held her head straight, face down, like a metal massage chair.

•

When Louise is brought to a recovery room, Janet spends most of her time sitting by Louise's bed, watching the nurses. They think they are so great, being loud with their fast walking and personalized scrubs with prints of soccer balls or lipstick kisses. But the nurses don't seem to be around when Janet has a question—when Janet sticks her head out of Louise's recovery room and looks down the hallway, they are nowhere in sight. Janet wants to ask them:

When will my daughter feel like eating?

When will she feel like keeping her eyes open?

When will she want to talk on the phone again to that imbecile, Claude?

When will she look like herself again, a cute girl with friends, a job, a nice-sized life, instead of this bandaged person who just lies there?

Louise's surgeon enters the room. Janet stands up and grins. So handsome, she thinks. She likes his trimmed brown beard and short curly hair. She knows all his outfits by now: his white doctor's coat over khakis; his blue wool suit with a pocket square; his blue-green operating outfit, a mask hanging around his neck.

The surgeon sits close to Louise and holds her hand. She cannot speak yet. Only one of her eyes is open. He tells Louise how well she did, how brave she was. A perfect patient, he says.

Janet's main job is to change the ice packs behind Louise's lower skull. It is time to change them again. She hurries down the hall to the ice machine and fills her shirtfront with more cubes. She empties the old ice in the bathroom sink and seals the new cubes in the plastic. The surgeon looks at her over his mask and smiles.

•

Tom has arranged that he and Michael will alternate meals with the parents. He will eat with Warner and Elizabeth one day, and Michael will eat with Janet. No one should ever have to eat alone.

Tom runs errands for everyone. He goes to the grocery store and brings back pretzels and fruit. He takes Janet to shops that sell lilac hand lotion and pretty notebooks, which she buys for Louise. He drives Warner to the drugstore to get sleeping pills, and then back to the same store to return them. Tom will give anyone a lift anywhere. Once, he gives a night nurse a ride home because her car won't start. Often, Tom sits with Louise, rubbing her cold feet for hours.

CHAPTER TWENTY-THREE

Louise is given steroids to keep the swelling of her brain down. They are making her psychotic. Warner cannot handle seeing his daughter talk to walls and laugh at chairs. Elizabeth sits beside her bed, begging her to eat a baby carrot. Louise thinks she is a supermodel, and that her stepmother is trying to sabotage her diet. Elizabeth tells Louise the carrot has zero calories, and Louise eats half. Warner reminds himself that it is all about numbers, levels, and that Louise's episodes are normal. The professionals know what they are doing. He says this again and again to himself. It does not help. He paces up and down the hallway. He hears Louise scream that her bikini line is already waxed.

•

Days later, a doctor they have never seen injects a numbing agent into Louise's left eyeball. He needs to sew a corner of it shut to prevent the cornea from drying out, he says. The eyelid, and the entire left side of Louise's face, is paralyzed—the result of disturbing the seventh cranial nerve in the surgery. Not surprising, the doctor says. They went in pretty deep. There are always bound to be a few unpredicted debilitations. Louise cries out from the eyeball shot and so does Janet, in her chair across the room.

CHAPTER TWENTY-FOUR

When I throw up in my hospital bed, there is a special way to clean it up. Two nurses roll me to one side of the bed, lift the sheet from the mattress, then roll me to the other side. They roll me again to tie the strings on my fresh hospital gown, and to put on a clean bottom sheet. I throw up about once an hour, because of the pain drugs, they say. One night I wake up to my mother standing over me. She says she is going back to her hotel room for the night, but before she leaves, could I please eat a granola bar? I must be so hungry, she says. It's been days. I am not hungry, but I take a bite, just to see her smile a little. I throw it up right after she leaves.

Wiping my face, a nurse tells me I look like an actress. The mermaid in that movie, the one with Tom Hanks. The nurse says she saw it on a rerun station. And I, with a turban of bandages, the gauze protecting an opening made with a small saw, believe her.

•

"The worst is over," everyone keeps saying. "You did it. It's all easy street from here. Everything's a breeze now."

•

For some reason I think Claude is here, somewhere in the hospital, waiting to take care of me. I call him on the phone my mother smuggled into the room for me. "I'm glad you're okay," he says. "But I have to go."

"Go where?"

"I'm at work." He sounds irritated. I imagine him holding the phone between his chin and his shoulder, busy, tapping a pencil.

I drop the phone to the floor and howl like I'm in pain, and a nurse comes in and gives me a shot. She scolds me for using a cell phone. The signals they receive and send can mess up the machines, she says. Everyone's main concern is: How did I get that phone? It is not allowed.

•

When the bandages are unwound from my head it takes a long time to get to the end. The unwinding happens in circles, and it takes so long I worry that my face will come off, too.

•

I still cannot tie my shoes or put my hair in a ponytail. I still cannot feed myself or bring a cup to my mouth with my right hand because my fingers are so stiff and the hand does not move and flex fluidly. My mother has been showering me. We have a waterproof wheelchair and use soap from the dispenser. I leave my underwear on for modesty. She uses a detachable showerhead to get my hair soaked. She wears galoshes. We freeze.

•

The surgeon tells my family that my cerebellum was disturbed by the surgery and so I will have problems with coordination and need to teach myself basic and fine motor skills again. I will also have trouble with my balance and walking. He tells them to remind me to be patient. "We will," they say, "we will."

A woman from physical rehabilitation wants me to get out of bed and walk down the hall. I cannot sit up without vomiting. Priests stop by, and I wave them off. I am moved out of my private room, out of intensive care to rehabilitation. "Yay, Louise," my family says.

•

I start out crawling. My physical therapist, who is handsome and Scottish, lifts me out of the wheelchair and onto the rehab gym's mat. He helps me get into a position I remember from Pilates mat class, on my hands and knees. He gets on the floor beside me and tells me to do what he does. We crawl. My family watches from folding chairs.

"You have to stand up," my physical therapist tells me. "We must teach your legs how to work again." To help, he straps on a safety belt: a thick nylon strap with a metal buckle. It is fastened around my waist, and he holds the strap taut with both hands. He tugs me up, and I rise for a moment and then tip sideways onto the mat. With my father gripping me on one side, the physical therapist on the other, I start to take steps. We have distance markers, like on a track. Ten seconds of staying upright is an accomplishment.

•

A roommate is moved into my room. She is very old and has lost control of her hands completely. They spasm and shake. She keeps the television on at all times, watching game shows like *Wheel of Fortune* and *Deal or No Deal*. Her son and his wife visit. They sit in chairs by the door. The son holds a bouquet of red plastic flowers. He has brought her these instead of the real ones so they won't die, he says. They leave soon, and she tries to cradle the bouquet in her arms.

•

My physical therapist comes to my room to get me twice a day. Mom and I are in love with him. He is newly married, but I still imagine myself as his wife. He and I do this strength exercise where I get on my hands and knees and lift one leg as high as I can, like a donkey. The physical therapist holds my hips firmly while we watch in the mirror. I'm wearing a sporty outfit Mom bought at the local department store. It's bright yellow nylon with a hood. I think of a wedding I was supposed to be in last week. I think of Claude. Screw him, I think.

•

To test my hand-eye coordination, I sit in front of a pegboard full of tiny lights, like Christmas tree decorations. I am to touch the light that comes up. My physical therapist times me. He counts the seconds it takes for me to touch the little bulbs. I try very hard to impress him. Sometimes I miss, and my finger will touch a spot an inch or two from the light. I get faster every day, he tells me.

•

After three weeks, my physical therapist says I am ready to try the home evaluation. The test begins in a room that has been outfitted to look like an apartment. It has a double bed with a chenille spread, a kitchenette with a two-burner stove, and a bathroom.

Five staff members crowd into the evaluation bathroom to watch me. I have to make it out of the wheelchair and into the chair that sits inside the tub. I get ready to go. Someone drops a pencil. It rolls by my foot. Everyone moves in closer.

It takes a minute to get out of the wheelchair, another minute to heave myself into the chair, and another to swing my legs over the tub. But I do it. Everyone claps. We move on to the kitchen so I can mix up some powdered soup and slice cookie dough out of a tube.

There is an old car in the rehab gym. I fasten and undo the seatbelt. I pass that section. I pass them all.

•

A resident comes to take out the staples that run down

the back of my scalp. The staples are put in a plastic bag for me to take home. They look like regular metal ones used for paper. They leave holes in my scalp that itch, and will keep itching, long after I go home.

CHAPTER TWENTY-FIVE

I t is decided that I will go to my father's house in Holland, Michigan, where the outpatient therapy is better than in my mother's small town. My mother cries and cries. My father and Elizabeth help me into the car, then fold up the wheelchair and put it in the trunk. The chair is new, they had to buy it at a store in the clinic. We all thought the surgery would resolve everything. No one thought there would be a need for one when I got out. Half my face is paralyzed. The right side of my body hardly moves. The surgery, everyone says, was a success.

PART THREE:
THE TREATMENT

CHAPTER TWENTY-SIX

Claude and Louise sit in the shady, quiet living room reading magazines. They are at Warner and Elizabeth's house in Michigan. This is uncomfortable for Claude.

He has not seen Louise for over a month. He flew into Michigan this morning and will stay for the weekend. Warner had met him at baggage claim while Louise waited in the car. They are trying to make it work.

She had looked worse than he expected. Slumped over in the passenger seat. Sunglasses on, one lens taped over. Only half her face smiling to greet him. He immediately wished he hadn't come. He sat in the backseat. She reached back to hold his hand. They held hands the whole drive, and he'd cried to himself, a mess of emotions, the whole thing a mess.

As they sit now, in the living room, Claude on the couch, Louise in her wheelchair, she is reaching for his hand again. All day she has been wanting to touch him, to hold on to his sleeve or stroke his hair. Claude wants to comfort her, but knows he needs to prepare her. That's why he did not go to the clinic for her surgeries, why he did not send her flowers. Why he cut all of their phone conversations short. He cannot see how it will work now. Will they have to build a ramp up to their third-floor apartment? Can you rent ramps? He doesn't see how it would happen.

But he can't break up with her with a bandage still on her head. He can't be the guy who ended it like this. He will have to wait until she is better.

What he tries not to think: She will be like this forever.

•

Louise has called all of her closest friends that still live in town and invited them to drop by the house to meet Claude. The girls, teachers and hairstylists, all blonde and pretty, sit around Louise and coo at her. They stroke her partly shaved head. They tell her she looks great, like the model with the tattoo on her scalp. They seem to be showing Claude how he should act. He shuts his eyes and pretends to be somewhere else, on a boat outside Santa Barbara, looking at the waves.

While they get ready for bed, Louise tries to kiss him. Her mouth feels strange. One side moves, the other side doesn't. She smells like disinfectant spray. He can see red dots on the insides of her elbows and wrists where needles have been. Her hip bones stick out when she leans against the bedroom wall to show him her new underwear. It is pink and triangular. She wants to have sex. Begs him. He tells her sex would be dangerous. He says he is sorry. He misses her body, the fit of their limbs. He is worried she will try to climb on him while he sleeps.

He lies awake the whole night, trying not to think, trying not to remember her tanned body on the beach in California, her energy, how she used to take him with her on errands Saturday mornings that would turn into whole days that felt like a vacation, full of foods bought at street stands and impulse purchases like a kite, or lingerie. He tries to push it out of his mind, how she used to look at him, how he thought she would always look at him, her bright blue eyes holding him, giving him courage, making him feel completely wanted.

•

At dinner the next night they have flank steak Warner has cooked, and Louise has trouble with her knife and fork. She makes a fist and grasps onto the knife and saws like she's cutting through wood, and holds her fork as if stamping a library book. Claude doesn't know whether he should help her, or pretend he doesn't see.

"Here, let me help you," Warner says. He takes her plate and starts cutting small bites. Louise holds up her right hand and flops it around. "Not good for much more than looks these days," she says, and everyone laughs. Claude wants to tell her to treat her hand with more respect, but Warner is staring at him. He is sawing her meat in quick jerks with a look that seems to say, This is how it works, buddy. This is what you do. Claude examines his fork as if seeing it for the first time, turning it over in his hand like a precious rock.

CHAPTER TWENTY-SEVEN

I cheated on Claude once. He'd already moved to California and I was still in Kansas, still in school, living with an opera singer who was as tall as a lumberjack. He had curly blond hair and credit card debt. We lived together because we were both friends with our other roommates, a short girl with a loud dog and a guy in pharmacy school who was rarely home. We had separate sets of friends, and he had a girlfriend—a pretty Asian girl who was also an opera singer. She went to the nail salon every single week. They practiced their arias on the porch sometimes. She was out of town the night it happened, and the opera singer and I decided to go out drinking, I'm not sure why.

He had a beard and it felt good to kiss him. Claude's face is very smooth and soft, softer than mine. The opera singer and I came home from the bar and had sex in his bedroom. It was filled with stolen furniture. He drove a delivery truck for a Danish store downtown and would sometimes deliver things to himself. He had a headboard, a dresser, a desk, and a set of matching bedside tables, all painted white and handle-less. Our other roommates might have been home. I didn't think about consequences back then.

Now that Claude is here I watch him sleep. I picture him in Montecito, leaning back in his office chair with a tie on, teasing the receptionist who has tan shoulders and a symmetrical smile. I picture him walking to lunch, squinting in the sunlight and jingling his keys.

The first night Claude and I spent at our new California apartment, on the floor squeezed into a single sleeping bag, all I could think about was that opera-singer roommate.

CHAPTER TWENTY-EIGHT

C laude leaves, and Louise is almost relieved. He kept telling her she was still sexy, her physical changes hardly noticeable. He was either lying to her or lying to himself, but either way, he spoke fiction. She wonders what else he is lying about.

Warner takes Louise to the optical shop. She needs glasses for her double vision: Walking around makes her so nauseated she rarely wants to go outside. Warner picks out a frame because Louise refuses to, and asks the employee to cover the left eye with tape. "No prescription?" the guy asks.

With her new glasses, Louise can write emails without every line blurring into the next. She can climb the stairs without getting dizzy. The doctors say Louise's eye could straighten out at any time—she could wake up one day and discover both her eyes gazing at the same thing. There is no way of knowing if this will happen for sure. All she can do is wait.

Because of damage from the surgeries, she also has nystagmus, or involuntary eye movement. Her left eye moves up and down very quickly, while her right eye moves with grace. The result is that everything appears bouncy. It worsens in darkness, and with alcohol consumption.

The covered eye is a mystery to people. Some people might think she has just had an eye surgery or some kind of temporary injury, and they will not stare or wonder. They will not guess she has had brain surgery. If they do not see

Louise try to smile, or walk, if they just see her sitting in a car, they will just think she is a girl with a vision problem, nothing more.

She calls Claude after dinner. He is in his car, on his way to LA to see some band. Yesterday he was night fishing with friends. The day before that, at a bonfire, drinking. Louise can't imagine herself doing any of these things. She can't even drink without her left eye leaping up and down violently. Claude says he does not want to give up on their relationship, but to Louise, him saying that means that he already has.

Louise goes back to a mirror and turns so only half her face shows. She puts on a necklace Claude gave her five months ago, a thin gold chain and a pretty brown stone. She applies lip gloss and mascara and ruffles her hair. She looks at that half in the mirror. There is still hope, she thinks.

CHAPTER TWENTY-NINE

Warner has a Zen rock garden that he combs with a special rake. The rake has widely spaced teeth. He makes dinner and does most of the grocery shopping. His painting studio is above a drugstore on their town's main street. It used to be a lawyer's office. A hospital bought one of his pieces. A hotel bought another.

Elizabeth is a financial analyst and works in the city. She cooks very well, specializing in desserts. She and Warner ride bikes together most Saturdays. She has a personal trainer who comes two mornings a week at six a.m. Elizabeth wants to feel useful, so she takes Louise to her hairdresser, who gently massages Louise's head, even the scarred part, in one of those special sinks full of warm water. They decide to cut her hair to a blunt, chin-length bob. It is soft and golden, and with all the layered ends cut off it looks like a child's haircut. Elizabeth takes Louise to get pedicures, manicures. She rents movies she thinks Louise might like, buys her bright pajamas, cozy slippers, and special ice cream that comes in small cartons.

Elizabeth likes doing these things for Louise. She has never had any children of her own, and she loves Louise and her brothers. Besides, Warner needs help. He worries.

"Should she go to therapy?" he's always asking. "A support group or something? What else? A meditation cushion?" He sits on the bed and rubs his face. He looks like he has aged ten years in the months since the surgeries: his hair now gray, a slouch evident.

"Sometimes I walk by a chair and she is just sitting there with her eyes closed," he says.

"Tomorrow I'll take her to my masseuse," Elizabeth says. "We'll go to the farmers' market. Get lunch. Also, there's a sidewalk sale."

She removes her eye makeup with a cotton ball.

•

Warner is relieved to know that an occupational therapist will help Louise. His daughter will learn to complete daily tasks with her right hand, such as:

—Brushing her hair and teeth
—Buttoning her shirt, tying her shoes
—Chopping vegetables
—Washing herself

She will have a team of occupational and physical therapists and a hearing-and-speech therapist. After the surgeries, she lost some of the hearing in her left ear. And because of the facial paralysis, some words are difficult for her to say, especially words that begin with "th" and "p"—"thistle" and "peanut." Warner notices it is hard for her to take a bite out of a sandwich because her facial muscles don't work on the right side. When she chews, she has to move the food from her cheek with her finger.

Warner remembers taking Louise to get donuts Saturday mornings when she was little, after Michael was born. He and Janet were still married. He wanted to make sure Louise still felt special, even with two baby brothers. Louise had been small for her age, six, and talked nonstop. She always chose the cake donuts with sprinkles, and Warner liked the bear claws. Once he taught her how to dip the donut in his coffee and eat it. She had spit it out and said, Daddy!

Tomorrow he will tell her about the article he read called "Recovery Foods." Beets are one.

•

The wheelchair is put away, folded up in a closet. Warner wants to get rid of it, but he is afraid.

•

The young woman who meets Warner and Louise in the waiting room is named Amber. She is a high school friend of Louise's, and Louise is surprised and embarrassed to see her here. Warner sees a flash of panic on her face and thinks, Oh no. But the two girls hug and use high-pitched voices that end on the upswing, like a question. He vaguely remembers this Amber. She was allowed to sleep over at boys' houses on weekends. Now she wears blue scrubs and is very tan. Warner listens to the girls talk about their old boyfriends, all dorks, apparently. When Amber finally takes Louise's arm and leads her back to the therapy area, Warner is relieved. He starts to sit back down, but a nurse tells him he is allowed to watch.

•

Amber gives Louise tests. She has Louise put wooden pegs into a board, circle words in a word search, make a paperclip chain. Louise bounces a rubber ball. They talk the entire time. Warner is mesmerized. Amber says she never left the area and is still friends with their high school crew. She is engaged and will move to Indiana after she is married. Louise tells Amber about Claude. Warner concentrates on not offering his point of view. He wants Louise to enjoy her time doing something different than being at home with him and Elizabeth. Some of the things Louise does at the rehab clinic:

—Stretching on a giant rubber ball
—Tug-of-war with a therapist
—Table tennis
—Playing the game Connect Four
—Playing cards
—Building towers of blocks

Louise seems bright and happy after therapy. She says it wasn't so bad. But the following week, Louise fakes a sore ankle and says she can't go. At Warner's, she sits and scoots to get up or down the stairs. She knows she can get away with it.

CHAPTER THIRTY

Louise,

Despite what you say about me abandoning you when things get rough, I'm still here and I still want to be a part of your life. I want you to know that I've considered many times quitting this job and moving out there to be with you and help you recover. While that would have eased both our pains in the short term, after a while I would have resented you, wrongly, for my having to leave my life. I just couldn't do that to either one of us. I think you and I are at our best when we're not being selfish.

When you say that I've changed, I had to. I hope that you one day understand the plight of having to sacrifice many priorities for the sake of a job. All this has made me feel very low about myself and made me question where I'm going.

I still cherish the idea of you coming back here one day. I want more than anything for us to again seek out the life we once planned for ourselves. We never went to San Francisco and Seattle together. We never went to Vancouver. We never went hiking. I wanted to.

Love,
Claude

Louise shows the letter to Warner and Elizabeth. They both repeat what they have been saying since Claude didn't come to the surgeries: Move on. When the time is right, you will find someone else.

Louise says, I know, I know, but in truth, she doesn't know at all.

CHAPTER THIRTY-ONE

Everyone thought Louise's double vision was temporary and would go away after the surgeries. But it didn't. So. At Amber's urging, Warner buys Louise thick workbooks of exercises, like "What's Wrong with This Picture?" and "Find the Word!" The exercises are supposed to help Louise rely on her vision more. Louise wonders what Claude, who does the crossword puzzle daily, would have to say about these workbooks. He used to fill them out in red ink and leave them in cafes for others to find. Louise would make fun of him loudly, calling him a show-off, and he'd blush and smile and try to get her out of the café before the other patrons turned around. Strange, how he's calling more than ever now, Louise thinks. They'd even Skyped a few nights ago. He'd bought another plane ticket right there, with her watching.

Her eyes are always sore now. She rubs them and uses drops. Overload, Amber says. It will go away. She twists her engagement ring around, which is her habit.

•

Warner is encouraged to see Louise doing small tests around the house. She tries to empty the dishwasher using only her right hand and keeps chipping the dishes. It's like one side of her body is conducted by puppet strings—each movement sudden and jerky. But at least she keeps going, Warner reminds himself. That's the important thing. She does not give up the fight.

One day Louise discovers that she can snap her right-hand fingers. Louise seems excited, and snaps for the rest of the afternoon. Warner tries to be happy, but he can't. This is just not enough to smile about. He wants his baby healed, now.

The next day Louise doesn't snap once, doesn't even mention it. Warner feels again as if they have really been doing nothing this whole time, nothing at all.

CHAPTER THIRTY-TWO

The Michigan rehab team gives me a face-shock kit. It comes in a black zippered carrying case in two parts. The gun-like part holds D batteries, and there is a thin piece of plastic extending from it that the therapists call a wand. It looks like a toilet-paper tube with a pencil sticking out of it. The wand has a black fabric-covered tip. The second piece is a box with a lever, which adjusts the voltage from one to ten. The two pieces are connected by a cord.

The idea is to touch the wand to the parts of my face that are paralyzed and to shock them into movement. Once the muscles are shocked enough and have moved enough by force, they will remember how to do it on their own. The surgeries damaged some of the facial nerves that control movement. I still have feeling on the paralyzed side of my face, so when I pull the trigger on the gun I feel it, like a sharp yank, and a flash of light behind my eyes. The therapist says this is lucky: Her husband has movement but no feeling, so he cannot tell if he has food on his cheek or is drooling. I envy him.

For about two months, I use the kit at least twice a day, and picture Claude, smoking, or turning a steering wheel, or I think of a photo of us at his graduation where we are arm in arm in our dress clothes and he is looking over at me, laughing, and I am smiling straight at the camera, my face moving so naturally. I shock and I shock and I shock, and the muscles move for a fraction of a second, then nothing.

•

I will not be talked into smiling for pictures—the asymmetry is too awful. The only way I will tolerate being in a photo is wearing my sunglasses, staring expressionlessly at the camera, my mouth a straight line, waiting for it all to be over.

CHAPTER THIRTY-THREE

C laude is back. Louise suggests that they go to the pool because it has steam rooms and saunas. Good towels and a smoothie bar. She wants Claude to see how much she's improving, how hard she's working. She can walk in the water! Without a cane! But Claude says he has not brought his bathing suit. Louise doesn't understand—she'd told him about her water exercises on the phone, and he said he wanted to see, to help her practice. Why doesn't he want to now? Why hasn't he thought of additional swimming moves that would be good for her to do, done some research on the computer?

She ends up screaming at him in the car on the way to the pool.

"I know this is hard for you to remember," he says. "But I have a job. I have other things in my life besides you."

Louise doesn't know how to respond. His complaints seem less and less real to her.

There is an Aquatic Exercises binder with instructions on techniques, and drawings. Her favorites are the Snow Angel, the Butterfly Flutter, and the Super Eight.

•

Claude sees the pool, greenish and still, through the glass door. All around them are echoes of people yelling, but he sees no one. He tells Louise to start without him.

"I just want to play a quick game of racquetball," he

says. He walks backward toward the hallway with the courts. Louise shouts, "But you don't have a racquet!"

Claude holds up a silver money clip, and waves it, flaglike.

"But I have this binder," she says.

"Five minutes," he says.

He jogs toward the courts.

•

We break up three days later over the phone, when he is back in California and I am in my bedroom in Michigan. I say the words and Claude doesn't disagree, but the last thing he says to me is, "Just remember that you ended this—that you did it" —and then he hangs up.

CHAPTER THIRTY-FOUR

Louise has started to admit that she will not go back to Santa Barbara. She will not be pursuing that dream of toasting champagne glasses with the rich and beautiful, of being part of some glittering crowd. In Montecito her face and body would be met with confusion by her newspaper boss, who hired her to cover dog shows and "Beat Hunger" 5Ks—how could she interview people with an eye patch on, clutching a cane? How could she eat tapas next to an aging supermodel, when it was hard enough to show her face to her own friends? People in Montecito do not want to be confronted with disability. They want to believe that perfection can be achieved by plastic surgery and the right agent.

Maybe she should get a job in a hospital, she thinks, and be a receptionist or an orderly. Or go to culinary school— she enjoys helping Elizabeth make pastries with spun-sugar wraps. She likes to read, so maybe there is something in that.

CHAPTER THIRTY-FIVE

Tom visits his sister at Warner's house. He is on summer vacation from college and wants to help.

Warner's house is twenty minutes from the beach, so Tom drives Louise there and they stick their plastic chairs in the sand. The winds are high, and tiny grains are blowing everywhere, but Louise wants to tan, so they stay.

Tom doesn't know how to talk to his sister anymore. Since she got sick, she doesn't want to hear anything positive. She shoots down any optimistic comment he makes, about anything, which was understandable for a while, but Tom had assumed that after the surgeries, her attitude would be better. If anything, it's worse. She's jealous of all her friends, their careers, their relationships—everyone but her seems to be moving into nicer and nicer apartments, moving up. They are all beautiful, every one of them, she says. Her bad eye bounces up and down as she complains.

Tom is three years younger than Louise, and three years older than Michael. Tom and Louise were in college together for one year, when Tom was a freshman. He tutored her in math. She became frustrated so easily, slamming the book shut and swiping it off the table. Tom has to be careful not to raise his voice to Louise in any manner. Sometimes, feeling brave, he asks Louise softly to please be a little pleasant.

At the beach, sitting stiffly in her fold-out chair, Louise says she wants to start driving again. She says that if she passes a special driver's education program for disabled people, she can get her license back.

"Paraplegics drive," she says. "I could get a handicapped pass and park anywhere I want."

Tom does not know if she should be thinking about handicapped passes.

•

Tom makes a corner of Warner and Elizabeth's basement into a painting studio for Louise. He arranges a card table with some watercolors in a plastic palette, a jar of brushes, and a short stool. Louise has not painted since she was a kid, but Tom did not know what else to do, and thought she might like it. She looks at the table, then looks at him, and goes back upstairs.

Warner is not doing much painting either. When he does work, he makes watercolors of the brain, giant and multi-colored. He walks around the house in socks while Louise watches the big TV screen. Tom gets depressed watching them. Elizabeth bakes pear tarts. She smiles a lot and brings home gifts. But nothing helps much.

Tom remembers when he was in middle school, seeing Louise, a teenager, pour vodka from their mother's liquor cabinet into a water bottle. It was a winter day after school, just them in the house, and the living room was filled with sunlight bouncing off snow. He'd been shy at that age, uninterested in team sports and skateboarding like all the other kids at school. Louise used to taunt him, ask him why he didn't have any friends and what he did all day. All he had done that day was walk in the living room and see her in the liquor cabinet, but she'd grabbed him, hard, and told him to shut up and go away, as if he'd been spying. He never told on her.

Another time, in college, Louise had invited him to a party. The apartment had been full of sweaty drunks, and Louise was wearing a sparkly tank top and lots of makeup. When she handed him a drink, he said no thanks. It was his first semester.

"You'll never make any friends here," she'd said, and handed the cup to someone else.

Tom does not want to remember these things. He wants to connect with his sister the way they used to, as kids, before she became a moody teenager, and then this. He would like to tell her about his new girlfriend. About his housemates at the scholarship house—a place where they all pitch in and do chores to keep the place running. But all Louise talks about is her physical therapist, her breakup with Claude, and how nothing will ever get better. "You don't believe that," he tells her. "Sometimes I do," she says. "And sometimes I don't."

•

In Michigan, the family goes to an animal shelter. A kitten will make Louise happier, everyone agrees. Louise will be responsible for feeding it, filling its water bowl, and scooping the small litter box. It is an experiment.

Louise chooses the cat that meows the loudest. A volunteer tells them the sad story of how the cat got there: It was put into a paper bag and thrown into the local river. A man walking his dog saw it happen and pulled the cat out. Louise smiles and kisses the cat's ears. Her wrists are already bleeding in little pricks from the cat's claws. She names it Ivan.

"Ivan the Terrible," she says.

Tom remembers the family cat they had to put to sleep. It had been attacked by a Rottweiler in their front yard and its intestines were on the outside, touching the grass. Janet had rushed it to the vet, and Warner took Tom and Michael to pick up Louise from a birthday party at the mall. Louise had been eleven, and came out holding a giant jawbreaker.

At the vet, Louise held the cat's paw, sobbing as it was injected. On the way home she held Tom's and Michael's hands in the backseat of the station wagon and stared out at the dark. Tom remembers her friendship bracelets and lace glove.

Now, Louise keeps the kitten in a small room in the

basement, away from Warner and Elizabeth's two older, bigger cats. She spends lots of time in that room. Sometimes Tom stands at the top of the stairs, listening to her talk to the kitten, even laughing at times. As he packs up to go back to school, Tom thinks, everything is okay now. Next time I see her, she will be stronger than ever before.

CHAPTER THIRTY-SIX

It is Louise's fifth month at her father's house in Michigan. Warner and Elizabeth go away for two days, leaving Louise alone. This is another experiment. For the first time since her illness, she makes herself coffee. She does her own laundry. She makes an omelet. At night, she locks up the house. She washes the dishes carefully, one at a time, soaping up each glass and plate and spoon and setting them all on a towel to dry. It is exhausting. It is a big step for her, everyone says. Learning to live alone will teach independence and instill confidence.

Right, Louise thinks. But my face still doesn't work.

Louise finds an old deck of tarot cards in the basement. She had been looking for something to guide her. She does not believe in God. She does not believe that Jesus or some other benevolent witness is watching. Jesus has failed her whole family, and for that reason, she decides to give the cards a try. Maybe there is an energy or force that ties all things together. Maybe the cards will help her see into the unknown. It has never been failure or rejection that scared Louise—it was always the unknown.

She learns how to do readings with a book: *The Everything Tarot Book: Discover Your Past, Present and Future: It's in the Cards!* She learns the different spread types: the Immediate Situation Three-Card spread, the Practical Advice Five-Card spread, and her favorite, the General Life Conditions spread. She practices them on her bed, well into the night. Her question is always the same: What happens next?

CHAPTER THIRTY-SEVEN

B ooks Louise has bought or been given:

— *How to Heal a Broken Heart in 20 Days*
— *The Purpose-Driven Life*
— *I Had Brain Surgery, What's Your Excuse?*
— *A Whole New Life: An Illness and a Healing*
— *Another Day in the Frontal Lobe: A Brain Surgeon Exposes Life on the Inside*
— *Don't Leave Me This Way, Or When I Get Back on My Feet You'll Be Sorry*

CHAPTER THIRTY-EIGHT

Louise calls Janet and announces that she is moving back to Kansas, to the college town where Tom lives. Janet is stunned. It's October, only six months since the craniotomies. Janet knows she still walks with a limp. Warner says Louise cannot stand up from a chair without tipping over, or sip water while walking. "I don't know about you living alone," Janet says. "Too late—I've already signed the lease," Louise says. "Well, you always were headstrong," Janet says, and realizes what a great thing it is, to be able to say that Louise is still Louise.

When Janet sees Louise on moving day morning, Louise is wearing the big, grey orthopedic shoes Janet ordered her. She is trying to be fashionable in dark jeans and a pretty blouse, big earrings, but her glasses are still taped. The left side of her face is still paralyzed. Janet strokes her daughter's hair, which is now shoulder-length and layered, and notices the scar from the incision, pink and shiny. Just be upbeat, Janet tells herself.

The whole family, Warner and Elizabeth included, spend the day moving Louise into her new apartment. "New" isn't the word, Janet thinks, as she looks around the wobbly complex with wood panels down the front, like a bib. The place is crammed with college kids probably not old enough to drink. Janet cannot picture Louise making friends with any of them. Every balcony is cluttered with miniature grills, stereo speakers, and empty beer bottles. Louise says she picked it because it is right next to the university where she will start classes soon, the same school she went to as an undergrad, but Janet wishes she would have tried a little harder to find a better place—maybe she could rent a room in a kindly professor's house? It's like she's trying to insert herself in her old, party-girl life again.

Louise roams the place happily, dragging herself along the walls. "Look, all the rooms are painted different colors! The bedroom is bright pink and the kitchen is electric blue! There's a closet, and over here a little shelf!"

Warner, Elizabeth, and Janet look at each other. Janet whispers, "What a dump."

Warner has brought books for Louise that he stacks on a sticky shelf: a self-budgeting workbook and pamphlets on home repair and personal safety. Elizabeth has pulled some items from their basement: towels, framed pictures, rugs. Tom carries the heaviest ends of mattresses and boxes. There isn't much to carry: a friend's couch, a lamp, some plastic dishes with roses on them. Janet puts on rubber gloves and cleans under the kitchen sink. Of course she finds mice turds and cockroaches.

No one wants to leave. They stand around in the little main room and talk, their voices echoing off the walls.

As Janet gives her a good-bye hug, she asks Louise if she has any food.

"We just ate," Louise says.

"I mean in the cupboards," Janet says. She takes Louise to the grocery store and they buy organic everything, cartons of eggs and bags of bright fruit. Once they are back and it all is put away, Janet has no choice but to go. Her new boyfriend tries to comfort her on the way back to their small town, but Janet just rests her forehead on the window. She keeps thinking of Louise sleeping in that place, and having to get up in it in the morning, alone.

•

Warner spends most of the moving day putting up blinds, touching up grout in the bathroom, checking the smoke alarm. He walks around the place with a large ruler, making sure all the pictures hang right. He still doesn't understand what Louise will do, really, or how she will do it. He feels as if Louise is a teenager leaving home for the first time, only worse. Warner does not really remember the first time Louise left home for college. She suddenly was just gone, and he'd never had to worry about her at all, not about drinking or smoking or grades or boys. Why is that? Why hadn't he worried?

As they drive away, he and Elizabeth glance through the rearview to see Louise bent over a box. Warner feels he is doing the wrong thing but keeps on driving away. He does not know what else to do.

CHAPTER THIRTY-NINE

Tom's scholarship house is a ten-minute walk away from Louise's new place. He often rides his bike to see her, propping it on the communal porch that's trashed with watery puke stains and soggy paper bags. Girls in tight jeans and pastel fleeces slam doors and run up and down the stairs, which are outside, like a fire escape. Sometimes, in the small, dead yard, a few guys without shirts grill hot dogs and drink from red plastic cups while a football game plays on the radio.

He remembers when Louise was a senior in college, and he was a freshman, living in a skyscraper-like dormitory full of guys who did things like blow pot smoke through dryer sheets. He didn't smoke, or drink, and wasn't making many friends. His roommate had a girlfriend, and they always were in the top bunk and under the covers together. Louise rarely called Tom, but one day she invited him over to her place for dinner. Tom was so happy that for once he did his homework without letting the sounds of sex distract him.

He'd been late. Spanish Club had run over, and he had to bike a long way with a giant bag of tortilla chips balanced on the handlebar. No one answered his knock. The door was open, and he ran up the stairs calling out, Sorry, sorry! but still no one answered. The place was huge—the largest room had a pool table, fluorescent lights, and a black-and-white checkered floor. In the kitchen piles of dirty dishes were everywhere. He had missed it. He'd checked his cell phone. No call.

The people in her new place are just like her old friends. But Tom cannot see his sister with any of these people now.

●

Tom takes Louise to the public indoor pool, which she hates by now. He knows this, but she at least goes—she won't go anywhere else to work out. Janet and Warner keep telling him that Louise needs to exercise every day, but she says walking outside on the sidewalk is humiliating, the gym is crowded, yoga class is too quiet. But at the pool Tom doesn't think she tries hard enough. She gets stiff and impossible after a few minutes and sinks to the bottom if he tells her to lie back and float. Her arms are thin but flabby, her tummy soft. She needs muscle, Janet and Warner say. Make her build it. It's the only way her walking is going to get better, the only way she'll get rid of that cane. Tom tries to show Louise the strengthening moves that are illustrated in her physical therapy binder, the strokes. His limbs are smooth and slow, as if swimming through gel. He demonstrates a Soccer Kick, a Bicycle, a Mermaid. He does the Boxing Punch. Louise's swimsuit—bright blue with skinny straps—looks bad. It was last used on a spring-break vacation to Jamaica where she paraded down the beach with her girlfriends. Now it sags and puckers. She holds a kickboard across her chest like it is a stuffed animal and sits on the gutter. Tom swims back and forth down the lane, hoping he is being a positive role model.

On the way home she doesn't look out of the car window. Not at the fraternity and sorority mansions with Olympian pillars, not at the man on a street corner meditating on a bed of nails, not even to see the people next to their car at any stoplight. She keeps her eyes on her hands. Tom notices that Louise now always wears sweatpants and bright T-shirts. Stretchy shorts. He wonders where all her real clothes went.

He asks her what's wrong, and she tells him about how, on her first night in town, after everyone left, she wanted to go out, but couldn't think of anyone to call except a guy she knew from the school newspaper who almost died from a bacterial infection. He had lost almost all of his fingers and toes and had prosthetics. In his specially outfitted car, they drove downtown to a bar and talked about how hard life was for them. Louise says they depressed each other, and that she hasn't called him since.

Tom doesn't know where Louise falls on the disability scale. She is not as bad as that guy, is she?

●

Janet and Warner call Tom early in the mornings, when he is still under his Mexican blanket, the room a dreamy dark. They ask questions about Louise, so many questions. They mail him checks so he and Louise can eat at tablecloth restaurants. Janet mentions she bought an air mattress for a weekend trip up. Tom isn't used to all this attention, all these gifts, all this contact with his parents. He tells them there's no need to visit. He has it under control. He is Louise's brother. He was there when she crumpled on the grass in Alabama. He can help now.

●

Tom's girlfriend, a short, motivated girl who is a teaching assistant for a human sexuality class, wants to meet Louise. She and Tom are both members of an experimental church called The Center. It is close to downtown in an old community rec center. Tom's girlfriend has cropped hair and does not wear bras or use deodorant. Tom has always liked how sweet his girlfriend is, how she gives everyone hugs and cheek kisses and remembers birthdays, but he is not sure she should meet Louise. Louise does not like to smile—because it makes the paralysis more noticeable, she says, which Tom supposes is true. Tom thinks that maybe, though, the three of them could watch a movie, or make some goals for Louise, write them on a marker board. They could get frozen yogurt.

Tom brings his girlfriend to Louise's place. They bring bags of vegetable juices, vitamins, and essential oils. The gifts seem to upset Louise—she leaves them, unopened, on the kitchen counter. Louise has prepared some sort of salad for dinner, and the conversation goes okay, Tom guesses, but honestly he was too nervous to remember what was said. They try to decide what game to play after dinner. His girlfriend suggests Pictionary. Tom says okay.

"Okay?" his girlfriend asks. "You hate Pictionary."

"I want to play what you want to play," he says.

"Don't be such a pushover," Louise says.

"Seriously," his girlfriend says. "Stand up for yourself."

Glad you're getting along, he thinks.

After the game, Tom tells Louise he has been seeing a therapist. Louise asks what they talk about. "A lot of things—school, my relationship—you," he says.

"Really? What does your therapist say about me?" Louise says.

"Nothing."

"Tom. Come on."

His girlfriend reaches for his hand.

"She says I shouldn't be afraid to tell you no. And to be honest with you about how self-pitying you are. Sometimes, I mean."

She starts petting her cat. "Tom. You don't know what real problems are."

He about flies out of his seat. "You have no idea what I do for you," he shouts. "How I defend you to my friends. How many parties I miss so that we can hang out!"

"You don't go to parties," Louise says.

His girlfriend puts her arm around him. She kisses his fingers. She rubs the back of his neck. Louise is staring with her one eye. He knows he shouldn't be doing romantic things in front of Louise. She always used to have a guy around who would lift her up and kiss her hard.

But he does not pull back.

CHAPTER FORTY

Tom takes me to an acupuncturist. It was his idea. He thinks my facial nerves might regenerate if the right spot is stimulated, if a needle worries it just right. I go along. Tom's optimism makes me want to believe it will work. We pull up to a renovated Victorian. It smells like a spa. Tom waits in the lobby with a plug-in fountain. The acupuncturist has me strip to my underwear and lie on my back. He puts little needles in my earlobes and pinkie toes and other places. After 30 minutes, he takes the needles out.

In the car, Tom asks me if I feel any different. "I feel buzzed," I say. Tom and I laugh. We decide to treat ourselves to whipped-cream coffees.

On the way I tell Tom that I still call Claude. There is silence. He guns past a spot. "Tom—" We swerve, and one wheel ends up on the curb.

"No more, Louise. No more Claude."

"I just want him to say he's sorry," I say. "I can feel that he is, I just want him to say it."

"Well he's not," Tom says. "You are not feeling that. What you are feeling is something else."

CHAPTER FORTY-ONE

Louise calls Davy, her old boyfriend. He doesn't answer and she leaves a message. She sits on the floor and blares the music Davy used to listen to, Iggy Pop and Lou Reed. She wears headphones. Tom visits, and she tells him she's working. "On what?" he shouts, but she turns up the volume until the sound is screaming, until her whole world is this. Tom leaves.

She thinks about a pink and white striped dress Davy picked out for her at a thrift store. It was made in the 1950s and had a full skirt and a tight bodice with thick straps. She wore it to classes with flip-flops. Davy used to wear old, slim-fit jeans and thin cowboy shirts with pearl buttons. They used to go to a bar made of cinder blocks on the edge of the county line. People in there had bare feet and shouted. Louise and Davy talked to everyone, sat with strangers. On quiet nights, they would sit on the futon in his apartment and look at art books. Davy's favorite artist was Hieronymus Bosch. He lived in the third floor of a run-down house. They called it the Tree House.

That summer, Louise had grown a Magic Garden in a shoe box. The display was paper cutouts that grew crystals when liquid was added. Overnight, it became an upright scene of trees and flowers with a prickly, tissue paper texture. They accidentally left the window open one morning, and when they returned that night, only skeletons of the trees remained. The tiny colored leaves and petals were scattered on the floor like real ones would have been after a storm.

Once Davy said to Louise, "I will never hurt you." She had thought it was a strange thing to say. She had never thought he would.

●

Davy gets back to her. He feels bad for her, she can tell by his tone, even though she dumped him for a guy named Claude. Davy says he'll take Louise to one of his guitar-playing gigs, that he'll come and pick her up in the camper.

●

Louise remembers the camper—she'd gone with Davy to pick it up at his father's place out in the country. It was parked between a bunch of four-wheelers and a wooden swingset. His dad was on his second round of kids.

She is nervous before their date. Her scar runs from the top of her scalp to the nape of her neck, so she wears her hair down, hoping it doesn't show. She waits on her building's steps.

Louise would sometimes drive the camper. The steering wheel was the size of a pizza and the seat was huge and leather, a captain's chair. They called it a spaceship. On weekend trips to Missouri or Arkansas, through national parks and hill country, they slept on the second story, in the cubby above the front seats. They'd leave the air-conditioning on all night. Once, they visited some friends of Davy's in Little Rock, a married couple who lived in a trailer with quilts and clipped coupons tacked on the walls. The woman had served baked chicken that was pink and bloody inside.

●

Louise shouldn't be drinking yet, but this is her first party since the Incident, and Davy is playing. He moves his body the way guitar players do, thrashing. He and the other musicians make bad jokes into the microphone and drink from the same bottle of whiskey.

After his set, he and Louise stand outside on the lawn. Louise tosses her cane into the bushes. Davy smiles and holds out his arm. He is a good person, with clothes that are purposefully a little too small. She turns her face so only the good side shows. He says she looks very thin. He says she is a poor thing, and waves to someone walking by. He pushes his yellow hair around. Louise wants to touch his hair but can't because of the cups they hold and the rule about touching an ex. Let them touch you first.

Now they are back in the camper. The wallpaper is peeling, and it smells like cheese snacks and dampness. She settles back on the couch, and sets her special glasses on the window ledge. This is better, she thinks. She has some great feelings. Davy remains in the passenger seat. Louise talks to the back of his head, asking him to remember karaoke night, how they made the whole audience cheer. She thinks that happened, anyway. He says nothing. She reminds him of how he liked to undress her in the camper and throw her clothes out the window. These are her best thoughts. He keeps his feet on the dashboard. It is getting a little light out. It is getting pretty bad. She sees his head on his knees. She kneels down beside the passenger seat and waits. "Davy?" she says quietly. He says this will never happen. He says he is sorry.

CHAPTER FORTY-TWO

Warner emails Louise the link to the Myers-Briggs personality test. He sets her up with someone in Kansas who finds her aptitude for certain careers. A librarian or some sort of nurse come up a lot. Warner encourages her when she talks of going to graduate school, seeing new physical therapists, starting a part-time job. He imagines her doing light clerical work, something that keeps her mind occupied, makes her feel productive. But he doesn't want to pressure her, doesn't want her to think she's not already succeeding. He waits for her phone calls and tries to be enthusiastic about whatever she's done that day.

Elizabeth mails Louise packages of inspirational books about women overcoming obstacles. She gets on the line with Warner when Louise calls, tells her the latest family news—who adopted a baby or whose birthday is coming up. She invites Louise to come back to Michigan for quick weekend trips, to see fine museum exhibits and eat in the best restaurants. Elizabeth wants to help Louise enjoy things.

•

Janet comes to visit Louise, and Louise suggests that they have a drink after dinner. On the walk to the bar Janet is worried that Louise, weaving all over the sidewalk, will fall. On a street corner Louise says, "Mom, would you mind if I had a cigarette? We're both adults, right?"

"Right," Janet says, and watches Louise light it, cupping

her hand in a practiced way.

After a few minutes of smoking, Louise says, "This is too weird, ha ha!" and throws the butt down and stomps on it. As they order drinks at the bar, Janet cannot think of what to say to her daughter. She would like to tell Louise about her new website at work, or maybe her house renovations, how she is painting the outside steps yellow. But when she looks at Louise, all she can do is wonder how she is really doing. She doesn't know if she can bear the answer. Louise is drinking gin and tonics very fast. She remembers the present she got for Louise's 23rd birthday, some comfortable clothes and a poster. "That's it?" she'd said. "This is my present?"

Every time Janet and Louise are together, whether out shopping or on their way to a doctor's appointment, Louise makes Janet follow a few steps behind her on the sidewalk. "How does my walk look?" she always asks, sometimes several times a day. Janet always answers with, "Better! Much better!" but in truth it is hard to tell. Louise cannot walk in a straight line, and her limp is still significant. But it might be better than three months ago, when she first moved into her own apartment. Janet wonders if Louise asks her friends how her walk is when she's out with them. She has friends, doesn't she?

•

Louise takes a recreational-therapy test called, "Recreation Is Where You Find It." It says she needs to resocialize herself. The directions are to check boxes marked Frequently, Occasionally, or Never, next to statements. One section is called Social Interaction, with questions like:

—I invite friends to visit my home
—I seek new friends
—I write letters
—I attend parties
—I attend club meetings
—I go to parades

—I argue
—I make social telephone calls
I never go to parades, Louise thinks to herself.
The test results say she needs to volunteer somewhere.
She could choose a hospital off the list. Other choices are:
the zoo, a meals-on-wheels van, a church daycare, or homes
of shut-ins.

•

Lately Janet has been talking a lot about her boyfriend,
the doctor, whom Louise does not like. Janet goes on and
on about how much she loves their after-dinner walks and
Saturday gardening. He's an Eagle Scout, she tells Louise.
"We never fight," she says. "He is so easygoing. Not like
your father, who would want dinner ready when he got
home every single night. Now we just both eat bread and
cheese if we feel like it."
Janet goes on. "His body is so warm. I could just snuggle
up to him for the rest of my life."
Louise does not like listening to this.
"How did you meet this guy?" Louise says to Janet on the
phone. She is lying on her bed, looking at the dirty ceiling.
"Your grandparents introduced us, he's their doctor, isn't
that funny?" Janet says.
Louise thinks that is weird. She thinks: You are not
allowed to have a boyfriend. She thinks: You should be 100
percent focused on your daughter's suffering. She wonders
what her mother would say if she said these things out loud.

•

Another quiz lands in Louise's inbox. It is titled,
"Spectator Appreciation" (check Frequently, Occasionally,
or Never):
—I watch television
—I attend movies

—I watch children play
—I travel or go sightseeing
—I go to a ball game
—I watch car racing
—I people watch
—I see stage plays
—I notice changes in buildings and landscapes

There is a list of activities organized into categories: Nature (appreciative), e.g., yard work, organized wilderness trips, county, state, and federal parks; or, Nature (sportsman), e.g., fishing (lake, stream), ice fishing, bow hunting, hunting, chartering a fishing boat, or taxidermy (you'll never know until you try it!); dating is under the Social Activities category, as is: Going to a coffee shop, waffle lunch, or having an at-home spa day. Louise has already thought about dating. She is trying to figure out who would want her now.

•

A therapist at the rehab center tells Louise to look in the mirror every morning and smile ten times. Your brain and body need to learn to communicate with each other again, he says. He tells her to take a third quiz. The quiz is called: "Do These Prevent You from Enjoying Life?"
— Often I don't feel like doing anything
— Work is the main priority
— I don't think leisure is important
—There won't be enough money for me to do what I want
— I won't have the physical skills
— I won't have enough free time
— I don't know what is going on or what is available
— There is no one to do things with
— Following through on my intentions is difficult
— Social situations are awkward for me
— I never feel well enough

All right all right! Louise thinks. Enough!

CHAPTER FORTY-THREE

Louise announces to Tom that she's going back to school in the spring. She's going to take writing classes, and apply for a Master of Fine Arts in creative writing, and probably volunteer somewhere, or maybe get a part-time job. But spring semester doesn't start for months, and as far as Tom can tell, she hasn't applied anywhere, or ever left the house. She spends all her time watching the students walk past and playing with her cat.

She is making a big pot of spaghetti with meat sauce. It is the first thing she has cooked in Kansas, as far as Tom knows, and he's encouraged. "It's Davy's favorite," she says, as she dumps a bottle of wine in the mix. She tells Tom that she and Davy hung out a few weeks ago, and she hasn't talked to him since. "I can't call again," she says, smooshing the sauce with a wooden spoon. "I've already called too many times." Tom gets out two bowls and two glasses of grape juice. Louise raises a shaky hand to Davy and sloshes some on the rug.

Tom is worried. He doesn't like it when he comes over for dinner and can tell that she has been in there all day. He can smell the wasted life as soon as he walks in the door. He tells her that tomorrow he has five appointments and sixteen things to do. One of them is taking a friend's baby to the park. Then he will wash the house's sheets. After that he will drive a van full of people to the roller rink. He asks if she wants to go with him.

"To the roller rink?" she asks.

She says they should save some spaghetti for Davy.

•

Two tornadoes tear apart the town. It hails, and small balls of ice break windowpanes and dent cars. Tom drives to Louise's door after the first one. He isn't supposed to be outside, but he has this vision of Louise just sitting in front of the television with her cat. He finds her standing in front of the window in the main room, watching the weather. They run to his car. The sky is yellow-green, the street silent. Everything is still. Then the sirens sound.

The next day they drive past Davy's house. The second story is just a shell, the rest already boarded up. They see the camper: it's in the yard, under a fallen tree and hacked in half.

Tom asks if she wants to see if anyone's inside.

"Keep driving," Louise says.

CHAPTER FORTY-FOUR

J anet would like Louise to move back in with her for a while. The apartment experience has been okay, but really. There are places in Janet's town where Louise could volunteer. That would be good. Janet would never tell Louise this, but she thinks that if Louise thought a little less about herself and a little more about others, she would not be so unhappy and tear-stained all the time. Louise needs to see people who are even worse off, she needs to exercise some empathy. Janet's new boyfriend is a doctor, so he could make sure all of Louise's sleeping, depression, and anti-anxiety prescriptions were filled. She hopes that Louise will start being friendly and talk to him soon.

Louise says no way is she going back to Iola.

CHAPTER FORTY-FIVE

Louise starts volunteering in a hospital. She hopes her mom is right, that helping other people who are suffering will snap her out of feeling so bad all the time.

She makes lab deliveries. She has to wear latex gloves. Volunteers are told to take the stairs when carrying lab specimens. Patients don't want to see fluids in containers and vials, especially when labeled with words like "CAUTION" and "HUMAN WASTE." They don't want to see urine, sometimes a dark, frightening color, sloshing around in jars with color-coded lids.

•

Conversation topics for volunteers are restricted to the weather or sports. This is under the supervisor's instructions. She wrote it on the marker board in orientation. Other topics that may seem harmless might upset patients.

Louise always starts out with the weather: what it has been like, what it is likely to be like, what it is like somewhere else. If she mentions that she is originally from Michigan, the news is met with surprise, pleasure, and many more questions: What is it like where you come from? Why are you here? Where are you going next?

CHAPTER FORTY-SIX

On a cross-country drive to Georgia to visit his parents, Claude passes through his college town in Kansas. He knows Louise has moved here. He wonders what she looks like now. He has not seen her for more than six months. He thinks maybe he will call her. Ask her to meet him for coffee, dinner, a drink. Louise used to be a wild girl. He would see her flirting with strangers in bars late at night—it used to make him jealous.

Even though he has slept with a few girls, he misses Louise, how she used to be, how they used to be together. Maybe Louise still likes vodka, maybe she still crumples those little square bar napkins one after another. Maybe she still has that brown purse, the one with metal studs all over it. It was the size of a grocery sack. Maybe they can just have a talk in her driveway, wherever that is. He can swing by, stand with his car door still open, engine on, bell dinging. It could be casual.

Over the phone Louise says yes, they can meet. Then she calls back and says no. She says no about eight times. Fine, no big deal, he says.

He stops in the town anyway, he needs to move his legs. He parks and gets out on the main street. His shirt is rumpled and open at the collar. He walks the downtown sidewalks exactly twice, looks in the windows of all the bars and shops, and doesn't recognize a face.

CHAPTER FORTY-SEVEN

Through all that has happened I always made hair appointments. I have kept it trimmed and light-colored. There is always someone who will do that for you. There is always someone who will ring up new clothes, cash your check, or point to the line where you sign a lease. There are people who will bring you food and clear away your dirty plates. You can pay someone to counsel you on your self-esteem, on your self-abuse. An eating, drinking, smoking, or sex problem. You can hire someone to help you exercise, or shop. You can have someone come in your house and organize your kitchen cupboards and bedroom closet. There are places that will take all of your old clothes and other things and give them to other people. You do not have to throw them away yourself. If you call a certain number, someone will tell you directions to anywhere, and if you look on the computer, you can see your apartment from a camera that shoots from space. You can go on dating websites and find potential partners. You can see their pictures. You can know their personalities, their weaknesses, even. But that is as far as it goes.

CHAPTER FORTY-EIGHT

J anet's doctor boyfriend has proposed. Her engagement ring is a band of blue diamonds, quite rare. They arrange a dinner with Louise, Tom, and Michael a few days before Christmas. The couple started dating soon after Louise's brain surgeries, which means they have only been together for eight months. Janet and the doctor stand up and announce their plans, and Louise gives the doctor a big hug. This surprises Janet. Maybe volunteering has helped her become more compassionate, she thinks.

"I'm expecting a call," Louise says, and plops her phone on the table.

Janet and the doctor discuss which songs and flowers will be featured at the wedding. They will serve a nontraditional cheesecake. Everyone nods approvingly. Louise checks her phone every other minute. Janet wonders who Louise could be waiting for—a friend? Some kind of date? Who can Louise date? Can she, even? What would the doctors say? Her therapist?

Janet wonders if she should have a talk with Louise. But any conversation about dating would be ridiculous because Janet does not have any advice for Louise. None at all.

•

In the middle of dessert Louise's phone rings. "I have a date!" she says after hanging up. Janet is relieved to see that this person in her daughter's mind really does exist, and that she is so excited, just like she used to be. But Janet is also very scared. She wonders what this guy is like. Why did he choose Louise? Who, besides them, her family, knows how to treat her? Who else can be good enough to her?

CHAPTER FORTY-NINE

H at Guy and I have a date. I met him in a writing class and he said that we should hang out. I hardly know him. I have heard he plays poker for money, gambles at kitchen tables in smoky rooms where people's animals are on chains in the side yard. I know that he skateboards and always wears a baseball hat. I'm not sure if I like him, but I cannot afford to be picky. No matter what anybody says, I am as bad as I think. Probably worse.

We go out to dinner, and I use his arm for balance. He holds it strong. Our waitress looks at us quizzically, like she is doing a silent logical equation. Maybe she thinks we are related. The waitress speaks loud and slow, until I say my order and she realizes that I can both hear and speak.

Hat Guy teaches me how to play Texas Hold'em at his apartment, in his bed. He wears his hat while we have sex, and when we are finished, he goes to the bathroom and throws up. He comes out and says he's not used to drinking so much. He falls asleep and I cry into the back of his hat. The next morning I start crying again, and he squeezes my shoulder and tells me I have nice, womanly curves. This makes me feel better. We drink soda from a two-liter bottle.

•

I tell my new friend Janey about Hat Guy, and she laughs so hard about his puking that take-out coffee explodes out of her mouth and all over the dashboard of my car. We are in the parking lot of a tattoo parlor. I take the bandage off my wrist, and little beads of blood are seeping through the ink. The tattoo is of two angel wings crossed at the bottom so that the shape is a heart. We got the idea from a necklace we saw minutes before at Urban Outfitters.

"This has got to be good for you, getting out there and sleeping with guys," she says. "It's recovery."

I think so, too. I've got to start somewhere.

"My mom could use your sense of humor," she says, re-doing her high ponytail in the visor mirror. Janey's mom is in the serious stages of multiple sclerosis and does not tell funny life stories. She lives halfway across the country, gets morphine shots every day, and is in a wheelchair. Her hair and teeth are almost gone. I found all this out the first day we spoke.

We were both taking a seminar on how to write a professional book review. One day I showed up with a bag of bagels because the class was so long, and there was a note on the door. The professor was sick and the classroom was empty, except for Janey, who was crying on a wooden desk. We left, and went out for brunch and had Bloody Marys, and she told me about her mom. I told her my story, too. "God, you're amazing," she said. "I think you're gorgeous. I can see it."

Her phone is always ringing. It rings while we're in the parking lot, talking about Hat Guy. "Hey lady!" she says into the receiver, which means it's her mother. She mouths to me. "Wanna talk to her?"

She always asks me this. And I always say no. I don't want to hear what that kind of sad sounds like.

●

I meet Hat Guy's friends. He takes me to a place with air hockey and he starts pounding beers and gets the hiccups. Some of the girls try to get me in a group photo. I refuse.

"Come on, Louise, what's the big deal?" Hat Guy says.

"You look fine." The girls have on thick black eyeliner and high heels, which I never will be able to walk in again.

I tell Hat Guy I don't like pictures of myself. He gulps his drink, and says, "Nobody notices your face. Nobody cares." He tugs me into the group. His tug tells me I'm not getting out of this. I link arms with someone I do not know. I make sure to look at the ground.

When we get back to his apartment he throws up again. With his baseball cap still on, he comes out of the bathroom and gets into bed. He calls me babe, and lets me take off the hat. He is bald underneath, with a fringe of hair around the bottom. He says his friends loved me. He doesn't say what he thinks about me though. He lies on his back and passes out.

●

Janey calls me late at night to sleep on my couch. She does this more and more. She wants some of the prescription pain pills that are left over from the surgeries. I give her more than I should. It is all I know to offer. We have morphed from girlfriends into something more like crippled dependents; there is no more charming or convincing each other of likability or goodness. No more compliments or caring conversation. She seems to expect me to always answer the phone or door, and I always do.

At restaurants she orders too many appetizers and expensive wine and pays for it all. She buys me gifts—one, a necklace of a stone hanging on a thin gold chain that I tangle. She lends me piles of books and clothes I might like. She kidnaps me: picks me up for a quick cup of coffee that turns into a scavenger hunt for the perfect pair of tiny jeans. We drive by the homes of her ex-boyfriends and just sit there, staring. I don't know what good I am doing her. I am scared that her mom will die. Then she will only have me.

●

Hat Guy keeps suggesting that we go jogging or bike riding or that I try skateboarding. "It will help you get better," he says. "How do you know you can't if you don't try?"

I wonder if he's noticed that I can't walk in a straight line. That I rise from a chair and nearly tip over. When I confide to him that being surrounded by pretty girls who wear eye shadow and dangly earrings makes me feel strange, he never responds. I don't wear accessories anymore—I don't want to draw attention to myself. I don't want people to look at me, ever. I don't know what people see, and this scares me.

Hat Guy refuses to acknowledge the extent of our physical differences. He only sees part of me. It's like he sees me, but squinting.

One night, on the phone, I end it.

"What?" he says. "Why? I thought we had a good thing going."

"I know," I say, "but I can't have you pretending that I am normal and will get better soon. It annoys me and I can't be annoyed anymore." I get off the phone.

What I am thinking is that after Claude, I can't be the pathetic one. I can't wonder why a guy is with me, is it guilt or pity, or is it real affection. I am not here to make a martyr out of anybody. That part of me was used up last time. The next guy I meet has to be made of different material.

CHAPTER FIFTY

L ouise is walking carefully down some campus steps with a hot lunch and holding on to the railing. She sees a blind woman coming up with a guide dog. They are taking the steps quickly. Louise tries to move over, shuffling sideways across the concrete until she can get a hand on the railing on the other side, but before she can make it the dog leaps up like a wolf and knocks her down. Then the dog steps on her as it goes on up the stairs. The dog does not bark, its tags just clink. The woman goes around. Louise's lasagna has spilled on her shirt. She feels like she should say something, but what would she say? I'm handicapped, too?

Sometimes Louise goes back to that same stairwell around lunchtime. She stands in the corner, waiting, and sure enough, close to noon, there they are, the woman and her seeing-eye dog, practically racing up the steps. Louise imagines lying down in their path, horizontal, making her body pencil-straight so she fits on a single stair. The dog's paws would punch her stomach and the woman would plant a shoe in her chest. Louise would get some satisfaction out of this. She would let them do it again and again and again. Thinking of this makes her think of Claude for some reason. It makes her laugh.

CHAPTER FIFTY-ONE

It is Halloween, and a guy named Nick is driving me and my friend Kelly home from a party. Kelly is an eighties girl and I am dressed as nothing. This guy is in a suit and a bow tie with a camera around his neck; he says he's supposed to be some historic photographer. He is a photographer in real life, too. He's cute, in a shaved-head sort of way. I like the stubble on his face and his voice, which is soft. We drive through the smashed-pumpkin streets.

He gets out and opens the car door for me and Kelly. I ask him not to watch as I walk up my building's stairs. I tell him it will take me a while. He says okay, and his eyes meet mine and do not look away, which startles me. I watch him drive off.

Kelly lives two houses down. She follows me up the stairs to make sure I don't fall.

The next day I email Nick a thank-you. I don't know his last name or where he lives, and I don't know what he knows about me. We have mutual friends, and I'm sure he's heard enough. A back-and-forth starts. On the road for his job, he sends me photos of his hotel rooms in Las Vegas or Dallas, and sometimes images of the sky. I try not to hope. I try.

•

A gold weight the size of a pinkie nail is sewn into my left eyelid. This is so my eyelid will close at night, if pulled down by a finger, and stay closed. "You have some real jewelry and you're not even married!" says my surgeon. He injects the movable half of my forehead with Botox, to match the paralyzed side. This isn't just cosmetic. He says the weak half might start moving if the strong side is stilled. "Motivate the little guys to do their job," the surgeon says. After a few days, my whole forehead stops moving. I try to wiggle my left eyebrow, the weak one. Nothing. The little guys seem to have given up for good.

My left eye is operated on again. The goal is to pull the pupil toward the center so I no longer see double. The dream is to get both of my eyes to gaze at the same thing at the same time. This will require multiple operations. After each one, we have to wait a few days for the stitches to dissolve to see if the surgery has worked.

I test myself. I lie on my bed and watch the ceiling fan rotate. I watch the yellow lines on the highway as my mother drives me back to the hospital for a checkup. Everything is still double. "Maybe next time," the surgeon always says.

There is some good news: My eyes appear less crossed now. This makes me happy, maybe happier than it should.

•

I learn that another girl likes Nick. She claims to be his best friend. Her name is Mallory, and one night out of the blue she calls me and invites me out for drinks.

We go to a biker bar. It is really a brand-new building with linoleum floors and posters of motorcycles on the walls. Nick is in Hawaii for a shoot—a college basketball tournament, Mallory tells me, which I already know from the emails. "I have him write down his traveling schedule for me," she says. "The guy can't take care of himself. I need to know when to feed him!"

I ask her if they're together, or ever were. She's sitting on my left, so I have to turn my whole head to see her.

"No, no," she says. "Nope. We're too close for that."

She is very cheerful.

I take big swallows of an icy gin and tonic. The windows are open and the wind is freezing. My hand aches from gripping the glass. Mallory asks me if there is anyone I like. I say no one. "Oh, I have the perfect friend for you!" she says. She means her roommate, who spends most of his time playing video games and hasn't had a girlfriend since high school.

On the way home, we drive by Nick's apartment building. "I decorated it, of course," she says, "beige and blue." She laughs, and I laugh, too, but we are not laughing at the same thing.

As she drops me off, she says, "Nick's just not really a girlfriend kind of guy, you know? He works too much. Besides, he's very picky."

I slam the car door. She isn't looking at me anymore.

CHAPTER FIFTY-TWO

I am scheduled for a facial reconstructive surgery, one that we hope will bring some mobility to the left side of my face. Before I go through that, I want to get the rest of my stuff from Claude's place. I want our lives separated, our ties permanently severed.

Two friends from college fly out to California and help me pack up my things. Claude has left for the afternoon because I do not want to see him. Claude has shoveled all of my belongings into a pile in the middle of the room. Tampons are mixed in with t-shirts and picture frames.

"Let's just get in and get out," one friend says, and I agree, but find myself wanting to look at everything.

I see Claude's dirty dishes, plates crusted with melted cheese, and bowls with graying milk and cereal bits. At the desk, I pick up a pile of hot pink sticky notes that could only have been mine. The bedroom is the same dark mess of purple sheets and a mattress, and I remember lying there, day after day, after returning from that Los Angeles hospital. One of my friends finds me in the bedroom closet and stops me from pulling all of the buttons off Claude's shirts.

I don't have Nick. I don't have Claude. I don't have anything but my own self-pity.

No, I tell myself. Don't.

•

The facial reconstructive surgeries happen in two parts. After the first, the nurse gives me a pass to go to the restaurant across the street. My mother wheels me across the street and into a restaurant. I'm starving, so she sets down a huge plate of club sandwiches with lots of bacon and mayonnaise and shiny french fries. The left side of my face is so weak that I have to hold my lips together in order to chew and swallow without food falling out. My mom doesn't say anything, not about this. She talks and talks so I won't have to.

Nick and I have been emailing this whole time. His jokes and little anecdotes make me laugh and forget everything else. While my mother's talking, a thought comes into my head: What if he was sitting across from me right now?

The strange thing is, the thought didn't make me any less happy. I will not give up like Mallory thinks I will. It is my time now.

CHAPTER FIFTY-THREE

M y therapist suggests that I ask Nick to lunch. She says lunch is no pressure. She says the only way to get rid of your fears is to confront them head-on.

The next day Nick is sitting across from me. We eat soup and salad and he tells me about his trip to Hawaii to photograph the college basketball tournament. He'd taken a picture of the head coach with no shirt on, and the picture made the front page of the city paper. "The coach called the paper and complained," Nick says. "He said his stomach looked flabby. Like that was my fault!"

When Nick laughs, it is a real, whole laugh, a laugh that enjoys itself and makes me smile, and for once I don't think about how my face looks.

But I can't help but remember Mallory. Maybe he's like this with everyone. When we say good-bye, I am still afraid.

•

The next day the phone rings and I say hello on the first ring. It's Mallory. She drives us to a small mall between two cornfields. All she talks about is Nick.

"I had to go over to Nick's the night he got back from the tournament and cook him something. I just knew he'd be sitting there, starving. His favorite food is macaroni and cheese. I make it a special way, but I can't share my secret!" she says.

I keep saying "cool" as I rifle through clothing racks, taking some dresses that I think might look good on me. Before

I make it to the dressing room I catch sight of myself in a mirrored wall, and turn away quickly, only to face another one. I put the clothes back. I was so stupid for thinking Nick would like me. He, an attractive, normal guy, deserves an attractive, normal girl. Someone who could buy a dress off a hanger and smile about it. He doesn't want someone hanging onto his arm for balance, somebody he has to worry about tripping down a rocky sidewalk.

We go to the shoe department, and I pick out some flats with straps.

"He's met my mom," Mallory says.

CHAPTER FIFTY-FOUR

A day later the phone rings. It's Nick. He wants to know if I'd like to go out. At night.

A real date.

When Nick pulls up, I find myself terrified that Mallory will be in the front seat.

After dinner we go to a bar, the kind with dartboards and scrawl on the walls. I almost get turned away because the bouncer thinks I'm drunk. A friend yells at the bouncer, "She had brain surgery, you idiot." Inside, I sink into a conversation with some friends and watch Nick laugh with his brother. Later, we head to the back patio to smoke, and Nick takes my hand to guide me down the steps. Someone says, "Whoa there, had too much to drink?" Another guy asks why my glasses are taped. He's drunk and loud. Nick squeezes my hand. "Want to go?" he asks. I say no. It's the truth. I want to be here. With him.

Nick didn't want to leave his camera in the car, so he's wearing it around his neck. A group of people ask him to take a picture. They all have their arms around each other. I know a few of them. "Do you want to get in?" Nick whispers. "No," I say. "Okay," he says, "I'll make this quick."

•

Pretty soon, the laundry, the grocery store, and weeknights have all turned into opportunities for Nick and me. He empties his pockets on top of my dresser at the end of the day. Mallory calls and invites me out for a smoothie. I sit across from her and we each suck our drinks and she talks about the new cupcake café and where to get a cheap pedicure. Then she says, "I'm really happy for you and Nick, you know?" I never hear from her again.

•

I need another surgery. Nerves from the tip of my tongue will be spliced and fused with ones in my left cheek. That way, when I push my tongue against the roof of my mouth, the paralyzed side will smile. That's the idea, anyway.

The surgery means two nights in a large hospital in Kansas City. I thought the surgery would be minor, so I told my father and Elizabeth not to come. The operation takes nine hours.

When I wake up in the hospital room my neck feels like a giant pillow. I look in a mirror and find a long gash of stitches that goes up one side of my neck and into my ear. It is crusted with blood and puffy like a snake is stuck inside. The left side of my face is yellow and beginning to bruise, and my bad eye is completely red.

I go to my mother's house in Iola to recover. I listen to chick-lit books on CD. My stepfather puts on rubber gloves from his doctor's bag and cleans the wound gently but firmly, wringing out the bloody sponge in the sink.

Nick wants to make a trip down, but I don't want him to see me like this.

A few hours later he is here, hugging me, kissing my cheeks, smearing my antibiotic ointment on his shirt. We go out for slushies. I'm having trouble finding things to talk about. He keeps asking me questions, and I keep trying not to cry.

"How can you even look at me?" I say. "I'm disgusting."

A bandage falls off my neck and lies face up on the console, looking like a piece of steak.

Nick says, "Hey hey, don't cry! You'll hurt your face." I

laugh at myself, gross, sniffing with a giant cup of red slushie in my hand.

"Things are going to get better for you," Nick says. "Whether it happens the way you want it to, or another way, I just want to be with you."

And the look on his face—I believe him.

•

The surgery doesn't work.

My surgeon is out of ideas. He says he's sorry. And honestly? I'm relieved.

•

Years later I go to an audiologist for a constant ringing in my ears. The results show moderate hearing loss in my left ear, which I already knew from teaching—when a student asks a question I must look at each face in the classroom until I can find whose mouth is moving.

The audiologist recommends a hearing aid, and as I hold the tiny machine in my palm, she points out its features. She says she doesn't understand why I hadn't come in until now. Didn't I want my quality of life to be all it could be?

To me, it already was.

EPILOGUE

It has been six years since the Incident. There are many improvements. The left side of my face sags less. My walk has less of a limp. I can do squats in my weight-lifting class, and even attempt yoga on occasion, using the wall for support. I can fold laundry with both hands, and possibly enjoy it more than the average person for this reason. I believe Nick when he tells me I'm prettiest with my hair pulled back so that my whole face is visible.

I suppose it would make me a better person if I said I no longer sat for pedicures, or favored hair salons that offer green tea and aromatherapy head massages. Why on earth do I still read gossip magazines? Why do I use whitening toothpaste, or ask Nick to pluck my eyebrows? Here's what it is: My face may no longer be classically symmetrical, but I still have the feeling of beauty. The feeling of beauty has nothing to do with perfection. It is about self-respect. It is about caring for oneself. I try to be a little less careless now. Being careless never felt right.

Nick and I are married now. We have a baby girl, Olive. Throughout my pregnancy I felt very self-conscious, unsure if people were staring because of my belly or my face, or both. Did people wonder if I should even be having kids? It hurts to think it, but I know that it will be a sad but inevitable day when our little girl asks about my face, my eye, the rest of it. She will realize that I look different from other mothers, that I cannot run after her in crowds, or find her easily on a playground, and I have to wonder if on some level she will resent me for it.

The other day Nick, Olive, and I were on a downtown sidewalk, squinting in the bright sun, thinking of getting coffees or maybe having tacos; it was that kind of day. I was pushing the stroller because it's nice to have the subtle extra balance. Nick said hello to a man and a woman walking toward us. "Nice to meet you," I said, and stuck out my hand. The strangers looked at me with puzzled expressions. "We've met many times," the man said. "We saw you just last month, at that party—"

"But we really didn't get a chance to talk," the woman said, shooting her husband a look.

Nick stayed quiet. He understood how stupid I felt, but also that there was nothing he could do. Before Olive, I would have pretended I was a ditz and bounced my palm against my forehead, not wanting to tell the couple that I'm not good at remembering faces because I have vision problems. Faces bob up and down, and I see double, so I rarely recognize a face until I have met the same person several times. But maybe that urge to denigrate myself is gone, or at least going away, because now, this time, I managed to raise my chin, smile my lopsided smile, and show these people my daughter, who was looking up at these strangers so seriously before breaking into a gummy smile.

Now I tend to let myself be looked at, despite the voice in my head that tells me to turn away. Maybe it is because I've realized that perfection is not what pleases the eye. What pleases the eye is what pleases the heart. My daughter looks to me for cues on how to act in this world, and I want to show her that you look people in the eye, you speak up, you stand as tall as your body will allow, and you say your name.

THANK YOU to my editor, Elizabeth Koch, for believing in this book, and for your vision that brought it to its best; I consider myself the luckiest girl in the world. To Lori Shine, Janna Rademacher, and everyone at Black Balloon Publishing for making this book what it is. To Devereaux Milburn and Nadxieli Nieto Hall, and the team at February Partners. To Deb Olin Unferth, an amazing role model who taught me how to be a writer and believed in this book from the start. To Mary Karr, for her generous reading and support. To Tom Lorenz, an incredible teacher, mentor, listener, and friend. Your constant encouragement means the world to me. To my supportive and inspiring teachers Joseph Harrington and Michael L. Johnson. To Jameelah Lang and Andy Anderegg, the best writers, readers, cheerleaders and friends all in one. To Kelly Schetzsle, Kelly Lemuir, Dana Bremner, Lindsay Metcalf, Corie Dugas, Cate Bachelder, Martina Bucci, and so many other friends: before, during, and after the craniotomies your friendship made it possible to keep on being myself, I am so lucky. To Uncle Charlie and Aunt Cheryl Stauffer, for helping me through those first scary days, to the rest of the Stauffer and Lynn families for their overwhelming support. To the Krug, Henry and Byrne families for their warmth and welcome. To all of my doctors, nurses, physical and occupational therapists, thanks for amazing care and such kindness. To my father, my mother, my stepmother, stepfather, and brothers, thanks for endless, endless patience and love. Lastly, to Nick and Olive, my husband and daughter, my life.

ABOUT THE AUTHOR At age twenty-two, Louise Krug suffered a ruptured cavernous angioma and underwent an emergency craniotomy that paralyzed half her body and left her with double vision. Now, six years later, Louise has astounded doctors and loved ones by recovering not only much of her vision and mobility, but a ferocious spirit and enviable grace. She currently lives with her husband Nick and daughter Olive in Lawrence, Kansas, where she's a PhD candidate and teacher.

Black Balloon

PUBLISHING